youth football coaching

DEVELOPING YOUR TEAM
THROUGH THE SEASON

SIMON JAY

Published by A & C Black Publishers Ltd
36 Soho Square, London W1D 3QY
www.acblack.com

ISBN 978 1 4081 1055 3

A CIP catalogue record for this book is available from the British Library.

Acknowledgements
Cover photograph © Shutterstock.com
Inside photographs © Simon Jay
Design © James Watson
Illustrations © Jeff Edwards
Editor Lucy Beevor

This book is produced using paper that is made from wood grown in managed, sustainable forests.
It is natural, renewable and recyclable. The logging and manufacturing processes conform to the
environmental regulations of the country of origin.

Typeset in 45 Helvetica Light by Palimpsest Book Production Limited,
Grangemouth, Stirlingshire

Printed and bound in China by C&C Offset Printing Co.

Contents

Session plans – contents

Key: TP – technical practice, SP – skills practice, FP – functional practice,
PoP – phase of play, SSG – small-sided game

Attacking and defending set pieces

Fitness conditioning

Introduction

Many people who coach or manage football teams have got into the role due to their own love of the game and their desire to help children improve their playing skills. Often they know what they want to achieve but are not equipped with the tools to meet their goals.

This book has been written to help coaches, parents or teachers working with 11-a-side soccer teams maximise both the time and effectiveness of their training sessions. The aim is to explain the reasons for, and benefits of, analysing team performance in matches, using this analysis to set a flexible training strategy based over the course of a season and allowing them to work on areas that need strengthening in a cohesive and structured manner. A comprehensive range of coaching 'session plans' are included within the book that a coach can use to fulfil their strategy and these are explained in detail to enable the coach to deliver a fun and professional training session to their team. These session plans are broken down into:

- technical sessions working on a player's individual technique;
- functional sessions for a small group of players within a particular part of the team;
- phases of play working on the team as a whole;
- small-sided games working on team strategy and structure.

Delivering these sorts of sessions can be daunting but the book will explain different coaching methods, terminology used, and how to deliver a comprehensive warm-up and cool-down before and after each session or game.

To ensure that this strategy is continuously focusing on the best needs of the team, the book will also explain how to monitor the effectiveness of the plan and how to adapt the strategy if necessary either for short-term periods to work on one particular area, or over a longer period to rework existing areas that still require attention.

While it is important to set a cohesive strategy and deliver quality training sessions, the coach should also know how to evaluate their own performance and this book will provide the tools for effectively assessing the delivery of a session and how it could be refined or improved when given in the future.

Finally, it is essential that everyone involved with the team knows what is required of them and this book will provide templates for player and parent codes of conduct, an overview of best practice for Child Protection, and how to recognise and deal with issues of child abuse and bullying.

The key aim is that this book will become an essential tool for coaches, parents and teachers to help them plan and deliver professional, structured training sessions, enabling their players to meet their full potential and to play at the highest level of football possible.

part one

stop shouting, start coaching

01

Why and how do you carry out a match assessment?

Whenever we watch a game of football, we always remember the contentious or memorable events. Everyone has an opinion on what occurred and why and, for a coach or manager, emotions, team or player expectations or personal experience can influence how they analyse these key events. How often have you heard a parent extolling the virtues of their child and their influence on the game yet you have viewed things quite differently?

As a coach, you need to be aware of this potential for bias in your own analysis of a player's or a team's performance and adopt practices that allow you to consider the game objectively. It is as important to remember why a goal was not scored as it is to remember why one was scored, or how the opposition won the ball in their own half and then missed a scoring chance, rather than remembering a mistake in your penalty area that led to a goal. Should you be planning your coaching sessions to remedy missing chances or to improve taking chances? Do you work on removing individual mistakes in the penalty area that may not happen that frequently, or on ball retention in the opposition's half and team structure if the ball is lost?

Research into what a coach observes in a game shows that less than 40 per cent of what happens prior to the goal is remembered and this decreases to less than 20 per cent for events other than goals (missed chances, poor passes, offside etc). Coaches will better remember events that involve their own team or players than those of the opposition and they will remember the events towards the end of each half rather than trends in the middle of the halves. This will set the tone for their subsequent analysis of the game.

So picture this scenario: your team has just won 4-3; your striker scored a great hat trick and missed a couple of other chances, you had two shots that hit the post and towards the end of the game the opposition pressed hard for the win, but you defended well and your keeper pulled off a couple of great saves to secure the win.

Or consider this: you have just won 4-3; your striker had better pace than the tall defenders and scored a hat-trick, however he was also through on goal on another three occasions and made the wrong decision. Frequently your midfield hit the ball long for the striker to run on to, but the ball kept going straight through to their keeper. Your other striker hit the post twice when he should have finished. The ball was frequently given up in midfield and they scored from two of these occasions. Finally, towards the end of the game, you kept hitting the ball long from the back; this was easily dealt with by the big, tall defenders who kept playing the ball back into your danger areas and this led to another goal. Only two great saves from the keeper secured you the win.

Based on the second scenario, you might plan to work on a series of sessions that start with 'transitioning from defence to attack', 'playing the ball out from the back', 'creating space in midfield', 'creative play in the final third' and, finally, 'finishing skills'. This could be done over a four or five week period and would work in a systematic manner on all the areas you have analysed as needing attention during your 4-3 win.

So, having made the decision to analyse your team's performance to give you a more systematic overview of its games, what are we looking to achieve? Firstly you must accept that in deciding to carry out the process of analysing your team, this cannot and should not be done over a single game. It is important to observe at least three games so that you can identify the trends of the team rather than the trends of a one-off performance. In one game, certain individuals may play exceptionally well, yet fail to maintain these standards; they may be faced by a weak opponent who does not push them, so their normal traits are masked, or different units on the pitch may not be put under pressure and therefore not show their traits, so the more analyses you carry out, the better. Also get into the habit of taking notes at games. If your left back keeps dropping to deep and playing everyone onside, make a note as this will supplement your match analysis and allow you to build a more structured picture of what is happening and which of your players are doing this. Finally, sit down as soon after the games as possible and write a review of the key things you remember. Be aware of the potential for bias as discussed above, but supplement your formal analysis with some additional notes of your own; if the opposition scored, can you note down what led to the goal, how your team scored etc, and this will build a picture of exactly what happened in the games.

Using our detailed match analysis, game notes and after-game review will help you to:

- understand the strengths and weaknesses of the team strategies and tactics for individual players, the team as a whole and the opposition team;
- allow you to diagnose key events in a match objectively and record the reasons as to the results of these events;
- allow you to plan and prioritise the team's objectives and set time frames for

this i.e. defensive shape can be addressed immediately, effective crossing is a medium-term aim;

- provide trends in performance such as scoring from corners or free kicks, and how a certain team formation works etc;
- show your team's performance across a period of time with objective comparison of how certain elements of the team's game have improved, i.e. shooting, dealing with crosses, retaining the ball.

Having gathered the information and analysed it, as a coach you will now be able to plan a structured coaching programme that will help build on your team's strengths and work on their weaknesses. However, even during games where you are not carrying out a detailed analysis of performance, keeping a record of key points will allow you to give more constructive feedback during your half-time talk and after games to review performance.

Analysing a match could be seen as a daunting process but, by using the following chart, you will be able to carry out a systematic analysis of a match, looking not only at your own team's performance, but also that of the opposition.

02

Planning for the season and measuring the results

Explanation of match analysis template

- **Entries into the attacking third** When the team in possession of the ball makes an entry into the attacking third and retains controlled possession for one or more touches, or when a set play is gained, i.e. a throw-in, free kick, corner etc.
- **Regaining possession in the attacking third** When a team regains possession of the ball from the defending team in its attacking third of the pitch in open play or via the winning of a free kick, corner or penalty.
- **Effective crosses** Crosses from wide positions that allow the team an opportunity to make an attempt on goal.
- **Non-effective crosses** Crosses from wide positions where possession of the ball is given to the opposition, i.e. the ball is claimed by the keeper, headed away, blocked or goes out of play.
- **Dribbling or turning attempts in the attacking and middle thirds** The number of successful and non-successful dribbling and turning attempts in the attacking and middle thirds of the pitch. A successful dribble or turn means the player or team retains possession of the ball or wins a set piece, a non-successful attempt means the ball is lost or a set piece is conceded.
- **Achieving set plays in the attacking third** Winning a throw-in, corner, free kick or penalty for the attacking team.
- **Attempts at goal but off target** Includes shots and headers that both miss the goal or hit the post or crossbar and shots that are blocked within one metre of the player.
- **Attempts at goal on target** Includes goals, efforts that are saved by the keeper or cleared off the line or are directly stopped by the opponent from entering the goal i.e. shots that are more than a metre from the attacking player who made the attempt.
- **Goals** Goals awarded by the referee.

| Match venue: | Kent Hill Sports Pavilion | | Team A (Home): City Rivers | | | |
| Match date: | 7th September 2010 | | Team B (Away): DC United | | | |
		First half	Sub-total	Second half	Sub-total	Total
Entries into the attacking third:	A	#### #### II	12	####	5	17
	B	#### IIII	9	#### IIII	9	18
Regaining possession in the attacking third:	A	IIII	4	III	3	7
	B	#### II	7	#### III	8	15
Effective crosses:	A	III	3	II	2	5
	B	II	2	II	2	4
Non-effective crosses:	A	#### I	6	III	3	9
	B	III	3	#### I	6	9
Dribbling (D) and turning (T) attempts in attacking and middle thirds: Successful (D)	A	#### #### I	11	####	5	16
	B	#### II	7	#### II	7	14
Unsuccessful (D)	A	#### IIII	9	#### I	6	15
	B	#### #### II	12	#### II	7	19
Successful (T)	A	#### ####	10	IIII	4	14
	B	#### ####	10	####	5	15
Unsuccessful (T)	A	#### III	8	####	5	13
	B	####	5	#### I	6	11
Achieving set plays in the attacking third:	A	#### #### II	12	####	5	17
	B	####	5	#### IIII	9	14
Off-target strikes at goal:	A	#### III	8	IIII	4	12
	B	III	3	#### II	7	10
On-target strikes at goal:	A	####	5	III	3	8
	B	II	2	#### III	8	10

Fig. 02:01 Match analysis chart

Match venue: _____
Match date: _____
Team A (Home): _____
Team B (Away): _____

		First half	Sub-total	Second half	Sub-total	Total
Entries into the attacking third:	A					
	B					
Regaining possession in the attacking third:	A					
	B					
Effective crosses:	A					
	B					
Non-effective crosses:	A					
	B					
Dribbling (D) and turning (T) attempts in attacking and middle thirds: Successful (D)	A B					
Unsuccessful (D)	A B					
Successful (T)	A B					
Unsuccessful (T)	A B					
Achieving set plays in the attacking third:	A					
	B					
Off-target strikes at goal:	A					
	B					
On-target strikes at goal:	A					
	B					

Match analysis template

Now that you have carried out your series of match analyses, you can start to look for the trends shown by the team and objectively prioritise the different areas of the game that need building on. Once you have this basic framework mapped out, you need to plan your training programme based on these findings and tailored to the age and ability or your players.

Planning for U11 or U12 players will need to be flexible enough to include modifications based on their rate of learning and understanding, and should include the ability to revisit areas to ensure such understanding is achieved. Planning for U17 or U18s can be more defined and include timed checks to ensure that full understanding has been achieved.

For the younger age groups it is especially difficult to plan far ahead, but as a coach you should still have your framework set out, so that as each milestone or section is achieved, you can then move on to the next section of learning. If you plan to have six weeks working on defensive techniques, but it takes you nine weeks to reach the level of attainment you are seeking, then it is at this point that you move on to your next coaching section.

So how do we use our match analysis to understand the trends, strengths and weaknesses of our team?

Using the sample match analysis in Fig. 02:01 we can deduce the following:

First half

The team we have analysed is City Rovers, the home team. In the first half we can see that we achieved nearly a 2:1 ratio of entries into the opposition's attacking third (25 for City against 14 for DC United) and when possession was lost, City Rovers regained possession eight times as opposed to DC United regaining it in five. There were 18 crosses attempted, with a 2:1 ratio of effective to non-effective crosses achieved. Both teams were comparable on the number of dribbling and turning attempts, but City Rovers achieved 33 per cent more set plays in the attacking half. In terms of attempts at goal, City Rovers had 13 compared to DC United's five. Most importantly, from these 13 efforts, City Rovers scored three goals, however, DC United scored two goals from their five attempts at goal.

This shows us that in the first half, City Rovers enjoyed a good percentage of possession and made numerous entries into the opposing attacking third, however 33 per cent of their crosses were ineffective and from their shooting opportunities, 60 per cent were off target, however from their five attempts on target they scored three goals. Defensively, they restricted the opposition from entering their attacking third, which means that they had a good shape in the first half and when the ball was won in the defending third, they either cleared the danger or played it out well as they restricted the opposition to regaining possession just five times.

Second half

In the second half, entries into the opposition's attacking third amounted to just 11 compared with the opposition's 20, so this was a 2:1 ratio in favour of the opposition. When possession was won, the opposition was allowed to regain it 13 times compared to five in the first half. Due to City Rovers' lack of entries into the opposition third, crosses were down to 11 but now the ratio of effective to non-effective was almost 50:50. Few set pieces were achieved, however the opposition secured 14 set pieces. Efforts on goal dropped to seven for United and again it was nearly a 50:50 split between those on target and off target but a goal was scored from one of these efforts. The opposition had 14 efforts at goal, but fortunately also only managed one goal so the game ended up with a 4-3 win to City Rovers.

So from this analysis, we can deduce the following:

Strengths

When the team keeps its structure, it effectively limits the opposition's entries into the defending third and when the ball is won, it is played out with control, either to safety or up the field of play. The team is able to achieve a high number of crosses into the attacking third and scores on average from every fourth effort at goal. The strikers and midfield work hard to win the ball back in the opposition third and are comfortable on the ball when they have possession, as their dribbling and turning marks show. The goalkeeper is of a high quality and works well with the defensive unit to deny the opposition efforts at goal or, when they are on target, this unit deals with the threat and concedes on average a goal on every seventh attempt.

Weaknesses

In the second half, the team lost its structure and allowed a significantly higher number of entries into the attacking third. Was this due to tiredness affecting concentration, thus affecting shape? Was it due to substitutions made? Was it due to over-confidence from a 3-1 lead? Or was it due to other factors seen? The team allowed the opposition to win the ball back in the defensive third more than double that of the first half. Was this due to trying to force clearances long, resulting in a higher number of set plays to the opposition, or again concentration and tiredness? While the number of crosses was high, in total 35 per cent were non-effective and this needs work; 66 per cent of efforts at goal were off target which could be due to poor technique, bad decision-making or, again, concentration and tiredness.

Trends

The team enjoyed the majority of entries into the attacking third in the first half and held its shape well defensively as it limited the opposition to few entries into its own attacking third. The number of crosses into the box was high but too high a percentage were ineffective and over two-thirds of the efforts at goal were off-target. Fitness levels seemed to drop off in the second half and decision-making under pressure was less effective in the second half. If the team can concentrate on keeping its shape both defensively and offensively in the second half, as it does in the first, it will find it easier to close out games, as it will have more control in the second half.

Using our notes from the game and our after-game review, we will now be able to fill in some more detail to the above.

The opposition's most dangerous player was its central midfielder, but we know he normally plays as a wide midfielder or striker and therefore, we got a lot of joy down the left of the pitch as the player they had there was weaker. Of the entries we made into the opposition's half, a high percentage were out wide so we played with good width and the numbers of attempted crosses, effective and ineffective, were high. Our left midfielder was responsible for the majority of the ineffective crosses and we need to work on this. In midfield, our two central players dominated the opposition and made a lot of attempted dribbles and turns, however they often took a touch too many and lost the ball when a simple pass was on. In tougher games this will be increased so, again, this is something to work on. Our strikers worked hard and won the ball back on a number of occasions and should be commended for this. One weakness was the fact that once the ball was played into our half, they stopped working and this gave the opposition some space in the middle third. We should look to work on the team's shape and positioning, so that, if the ball is lost, one of them drops into midfield to give us compactness and balance, with one staying high to offer an outlet.

In the second half, the opposition moved the danger player from midfield to upfront and he was responsible for winning the ball back on a lot of occasions with his speed and work rate. Our defenders got caught a few times playing with their heads down and also didn't move to offer simple outlets to recycle the ball, so we need to work on this area. The keeper also needed to keep up his communication to warn of the threat from the striker and if necessary call for a quick clearance. Having said this, a number of times the ball was cleared off the pitch when players had more time than they understood and again we need to work on communication. Our substitutions also caused the team to lose its shape and impetus, so the coach needs to be aware of this and look to substitute in a more structured manner.

Summary
Looking at the statistics of the match analysis and our personal notes from the game, now we can get a really good feel for the strengths, weaknesses and trends

of the team and methodically put together a training schedule that will work on the weaknesses and build on the strengths.

Starting the planning?

Different coaches have different philosophies. When Kevin Keegan managed Newcastle United for the first time, his philosophy very much seemed to be, 'we don't care how many you score, we will score more'. Other managers take the approach of 'we will stop you scoring and get one ourselves' – George Graham's Arsenal of the 1990s was very much built to this mould. In the modern era, Arsene Wenger's Arsenal side is one of the most entertaining teams in Europe, whereas Jose Mourinho's Chelsea team was functional and ground out wins. Your own personal philosophy will determine how you wish to start your planning. For the purpose of explaining how to set out our season-long framework, we will begin with our sample team's defensive frailties, move on to our midfield possession and finish with our attacking structure and finishing skills.

Planning framework

To allow us to set out our coaching plan, we can use the Coaching Framework Template that follows.

- **Dates** Firstly, we have filled in the dates when we train (for our sample team this is midweek on a Wednesday) and the dates when the team will be assessed using the Match Analysis sheets (Sundays).
- **Period** We then fill in the period of the season we are in; August will be pre-season training, September through April will be the league and cup competitions, May will be the beginning of the summer tournament phase, with June and July as rest periods for the team.
- **Themes** This is the section where we put down what areas of the team's game we are going to work on, e.g. August is pre-season training and so we are going to be working on physical preparation and tactical responsibilities.
- **Practical content** Here we list in more detail the areas we are going to work on and how.
- **Planned evaluation** Here we note down when we will assess the team again to ensure we are meeting the objectives we have set ourselves. If we have, we can move on to the next 'Theme', if we haven't, this is the time to modify our Coaching Framework so that we can revisit the 'Theme' we have just completed and carry out some more coaching to ensure all the players understand practical content.

Table 1

	August				September					October				November				December				
Date	5	12	19	26	2	9	16	23	30	7	14	21	28	4	11	18	25	2	9	16	23	30
Period	Pre-season				League, season and cup competitions																	
Themes	Physical preparation and tactical responsibilities				Defensive technical development and tactical responsibilities					Creating space and ball retention in midfield				Creating chances and finishing				Set pieces				
Practical content	Speed and aerobic endurance, attacking and defending as a unit through SSGs				SSGs, PoP and functional practice working on defending, plus technical practice for GK					Technical practice, SSGs, PoP and functional practice working on midfield unit				Functional practice, PoP and SSGs working on wide players and strikers unit				Functional practice working on attacking and defending corners, free kicks and throw-ins				
Planned evaluation				30					30				04				01					06

Table 2

	January				February				March				April					May				
Date	7	14	21	28	4	11	18	25	4	11	18	25	1	8	15	22	29	6	13	20	27	
Period	League, season and cup competitions																	End-of-season and beginning-of-summer tournaments				
Themes	Defensive pressing or holding plus quick counter-attacking				Ball and player movement				Improvising and finishing				Individual ball skills and control					SSG game preparation for summer tournament				
Practical content	SSGs and PoPs working on defensive shape, followed by quick counter-attacking				SSGs and PoPs working on playing out from the back, ball retention and recycling, followed by player movement to create space				SSGs and PoPs working on individual and group improvisation and creative play				Coever-type technical drills for the individual and units to work on ball skills					SSGs working combined play (6 v 6) and team structure				
Planned evaluation				04				01				01					04				02	

Fig. 02:02 Coaching framework sample

	August	September	October	November	December
Date					
Period					
Themes					
Practical content					
Planned evaluation					

	January	February	March	April	May
Date					
Period					
Themes					
Practical content					
Planned evaluation					

Coaching framework template

As our sample team will begin training in early August, our emphasis in this phase of the plan is on building fitness levels and starting to introduce team structure back into the minds of the players. You may have new players joining your team who need to understand how you wish to structure your team's shape, or you may have lost players and need to move other players around to fill the spaces made vacant; doing this in a structured manner through the pre-season phase will allow all players to understand fully what is required of them.

Building fitness levels can be accomplished in a variety of ways, from running laps around the pitch, to carrying out the training techniques as explained in Fitness Conditioning, p.136, such as circuit training, Fartlek runs, shuttle runs, pyramid runs etc. Especially for younger players, you should try to make the building of fitness levels fun. Even for older players, taking the monotony out of fitness training will lead to a happier group of players and more enjoyment of training sessions. Try small-sided games (3 v 3 or 4 v 4) played at a fast pace with penalties for lack of effort (e.g. 10 star jumps) for players not moving. Group your players into three teams, have two playing and one team doing circuits around the SSG pitch, sprinting down the short or long sides and recovery runs down the other and then, after a set time (e.g. three minutes) swap the losing team to the outside runs – you will be amazed at how hard they work in the game to avoid the outside runs, but in fact they are working just as hard playing.

In our fictional team, we have identified that we wish to concentrate on 'defensive technical development and tactical responsibilities'. This will involve technical coaching sessions, functional practices, phases of play (PoP) and small-sided games (SSG), in fact all the different types of coaching sessions we have. We will also concentrate in September on technical practices for the goalkeeper.

We carry on filling in each month until we have completed the season-long coaching plan, making sure we have scheduled in regular assessments so that we can measure the progress the team is making and be confident that the team has fully understood the theme before moving on to the next stage.

Once our coaching framework is completed, we need to drill down and plan to a higher degree for each month. You may wish to complete each month in one go, or you may decide to complete the first month and carry out your evaluation so that you can be sure the theme has been understood before moving on to the next: the choice is yours. To help explain the concept, we have prepared the monthly plans for August, September and October for our team and included a monthly plan template for your future use.

Now that you have completed your match analysis, understand your team's strengths and weaknesses, planned your coaching framework for the season and prepared your monthly detailed plan, you're ready to begin the coaching.

Month:	August
Period:	Pre-season
Themes:	Physical preparation and tactical responsibilities
Practical content:	Speed and aerobic endurance, attacking and defending as a unit through SSGs

Session date:	5th August	
1	Dynamic warm-up building in intensity towards fitness work	10 mins
2	Bleep test	20 mins
3	5 v 5 SSG – 3 teams, 2 playing, 1 sprints short side of SSG pitch	18 mins
4	7 v 7 SSG – defensive roles and responsibilities	20 mins
5	Cool-down	7 mins

Session date:	12th August	
1	Dynamic warm-up building in intensity towards fitness work	10 mins
2	Fartlek runs	20 mins
3	3 groups of 5 – pass and move cones	18 mins
4	7 v 7 SSG – creating space	20 mins
5	Cool-down	7 mins

Session date:	19th August	
1	Dynamic warm-up building in intensity towards fitness work	10 mins
2	Pyramid runs	20 mins
3	Paired sprint training	18 mins
4	7 v 7 SSG – marking players and tracking runners	20 mins
5	Cool-down	7 mins

Session date:	26th August	
1	Dynamic warm-up building in intensity towards fitness work	10 mins
2	Bleep test	20 mins
3	Aerobic endurance – 7 v 7, 2 touch, pass and move	18 mins
4	7 v 7 SSG – changing the direction of play	20 mins
5	Cool-down	7 mins

Evaluation date:	Ongoing through sessions, record bleep test results
Evaluation result:	Bleep test results from 26th showed in all cases an improvement on results from bleep test on 5th. Visible signs of anaerobic and aerobic fitness improvements through latter sessions.

Fig. 02:03 Monthly session planner 1

Month:	September
Period:	League, season and cup competitions
Themes:	Defensive technical development and tactical responsibilities
Practical content:	SSGs, PoP and functional practice working on defending, plus technical practice for GK

Session date:	2nd September	
1	Dynamic warm-up	10 mins
2	5 v 5 SSG – 2 teams high intensity GK – Dealing with crosses	20 mins
3	Technical practice – defending triangle	20 mins
4	PoP – roles and responsibilities in the defensive third	20 mins
5	Cool-down	5 mins

Session date:	9th September	
1	Dynamic warm-up	10 mins
2	5 v 5 SSG – 2 teams high intensity GK – narrowing the angle	20 mins
3	Technical practice – making play predictable	20 mins
4	SSG – mental concentration and denying space	20 mins
5	Cool-down	5 mins

Session date:	16th September	
1	Dynamic warm-up	10 mins
2	Paired sprint work and shooting GK – distribution	20 mins
3	Technical practice – 2 v 2 defending	20 mins
4	Functional practice – tracking runners	20 mins
5	Cool-down	5 mins

Session date:	23rd September	
1	Dynamic warm-up	10 mins
2	Defensive heading GK – shot stopping	20 mins
3	Technical practice – recovery runs	20 mins
4	SSG – pressing the ball or dropping to be compact	20 mins
5	Cool-down	5 mins

Session date:	30th September	
1	Dynamic warm-up	10 mins
2	SSG – dealing with crosses	20 mins
3	PoP – dealing with the back pass and distribution	20 mins
4	SSG – defensive organisation and shape	20 mins
5	Cool-down	5 mins

Evaluation date:	4th October
Evaluation result:	*Team had a much better shape, limited the opposition in their entries into the defending third and made good use of the ball when won – revisit roles and responsibilities next week to ensure midfield players fully understand their roles when tracking and marking midfield runners and screening strikers.*

Fig. 02:04 Monthly session planner 2

Month:	October	
Period:	League, season and cup competitions	
Themes:	Creating space and ball retention in midfield	
Practical content:	Technical practice, SSGs, PoP and functional practice working on the midfield unit	
Session date:	7th October	
1 Dynamic warm-up		10 mins
2 Paired players – turning practice (ball manipulation)		15 mins
3 Technical practice – maintaining possession		20 mins
4 SSG – development of play from the defending third		20 mins
5 Cool-down		5 mins
Session date:	14th October	
1 Dynamic warm-up		10 mins
2 Paired players – turning practice (ball manipulation)		15 mins
3 Technical practice – maintaining possession progression		20 mins
4 PoP – creating space in the middle third		20 mins
5 Cool-down		5 mins
Session date:	21st October	
1 Dynamic warm-up		10 mins
2 Paired players – turning practice (ball manipulation)		15 mins
3 Functional practice – responsibilities of a wide player		20 mins
4 SSG – quick interplay and passing		20 mins
5 Cool-down		5 mins
Session date:	28th October	
1 Dynamic warm-up		10 mins
2 Paired players – turning practice (ball manipulation)		15 mins
3 Functional practice – delivering crosses		20 mins
4 PoP – movement, receiving and turning		20 mins
5 Cool-down		5 mins
Evaluation date:	1st November	
Evaluation result:		

Fig. 02:05 Monthly session planner 3

Month:	
Period:	
Themes:	
Practical content:	
Session date:	
Session date:	
Session date:	
Session date:	
Evaluation date:	
Evaluation result:	

Monthly session planner template

Principles of coaching and teaching

The key thing for any coach is to promote a positive learning environment so that they get the best out of their players while making the practices safe, fun and rewarding. To achieve this, it is important that the coach understands the strategies and styles necessary to promote effective learning. Simply running practice session after practice session will not ensure players learn and progress if the coach does not fully understand how players are absorbing this information.

It is also vitally important to create a positive learning environment through thorough planning and preparation, setting the right example to the players in terms of dress code and appearance, punctuality, enthusiasm and language, all of which sets the correct tone for the session you want to deliver.

Your next challenge is to plan and prepare sessions that motivate the players to want to learn; sessions that are challenging and varied and mean the players look forward to coming to training. Players will soon realise if a session is poorly planned and will quickly lose interest if the session is boring; this will inevitably lead to behavioural issues that can disrupt the whole group.

How do we create this positive learning environment? Below are a few suggestions.

- Prior to arriving at your practice session, ensure you have planned how the session will run, what topics and themes you are going to work on, have prepared your session plan and have all the equipment necessary to deliver the session.
- If possible, set up before the session starts, mark out your coaching areas, arrange your sets of bibs, check the balls are all inflated, and check the playing area and equipment are safe.
- Prepare a safety zone where all unused kit and players' clothing, bags etc can be placed to ensure nothing can enter the playing or training area and cause a safety hazard.
- Prior to starting your coaching session, explain to the players the topics you are going to cover, the time you have allowed for each part of the session and the aims and goals of what you want them to learn.
- During the session, try to provide positive feedback on players' individual

development and progression, and deliver positive feedback on their performance in a way that does not undermine their competence but, where necessary,
corrects areas that need correcting.

- Aim to make the sessions varied and challenging, test the players' competencies and push them outside their comfort zones.
- Ensure your sessions involve realistic situations such as small-sided games
and phases of play that are competitive and make the players bring a game
type mentality to their training – remember the old adage 'you play how you
train'.
- Include practices that monitor progression such as fitness tests (bleep tests,
sprint tests, Cooper tests – see session plan 84) for older players or timed
running with the ball, turns through cones etc for younger players.
- Give praise to all players who are doing well in terms of effort or technique.
- Treat the players as individuals, talk to them about their thoughts on the sessions,
about the team and about their own aspirations.
- Provide feedback on a formal basis at planned intervals such as a mid-season
feedback sheet, outlining what level you feel they are currently, what level they
should be looking to reach, and targets or goals on how to do this. Make the
player understand that you have their long-term interests at heart and are not
just interested in next week's result.
- Aim to bring the best out of all your players using a range of techniques and
coaching styles and through the structured approach of long-term planning to
bring variety to all your sessions.

Getting the best from your players

Players pick up information in a variety of ways and each member of your squad
will have a different method for learning things: some will prefer to be shown how
to do something; others will prefer to do it themselves and ask for feedback; some
will like to have a technique explained; others will copy their peers. As a coach
you need to understand these different methods and then utilise them all to deliver
a session. Having said this, though, remember people learn best when they become
actively involved in the learning experience, for example, when they recognise for
themselves where a skill or technique should be used (through either seeing it
happen live in a game or on the telly); when they can call on previous examples
of coaching and then learn a new technique that builds on this, i.e. defending
triangle and then forcing play in one direction (see session plans 11 and 12);
when they are enjoying what they are doing; and, most importantly, when they can
see they are making improvements.

It is also important to understand the principles of how players will learn. If you
want to emphasise some basic techniques like how to control the ball with a certain

part of the foot, set the practice up to have numerous repetitions. Then you can check that all the players fully understand the concept and practise this until the objective is met. If you want to ensure that something is fully understood and fully absorbed, set up shorter and frequent practices to aid long-term learning. For example with the defensive triangle, revisit it for a short period over four or five weeks and then build on this principle with small progressions over another four or five weeks. This will ensure that the principles are retained more successfully. If coaching young players, anything over 15 minutes in length can lead to them becoming bored and tired; remember, if you are coaching on a week night, they will probably have had a full day at school and you need to keep it short, interesting and fun. For older players, you can lengthen the session to include more learning points, but again get these points over quickly and let them play. Finally, make the practices varied and interesting, a line drill on shooting where each player has to wait for the other members of the squad to have a go will not get the best out of them.

Next you need to think about how to deliver your coaching points. Before asking your players to perform a technique – show them. If it is complicated, break it down into smaller chunks. Once you have shown them via a demonstration of what you want to achieve, let them do it – move from a demonstration to practice as soon as possible. As a rule of thumb, try and keep your demonstrations down to 30 seconds or shorter, any longer than this and you will see the players' legs lock, arms will cross and they will begin to listen less. Make sure you perform the demonstration to the skill level of the players; if you set the level to high, the players will not fully understand what you are coaching, too low and they will become bored. Finally, make sure you demonstrate frequently to ensure they fully understand. If certain players have got the skill mastered, but others haven't, split them up. You may tell the ones who have mastered it to try something more advanced to keep them focused while you take the others aside and show them again, slowing it down to better demonstrate.

When giving instructions, remember:

- don't overload the players with too much information;
- keep the instructions down to one or two points;
- use the instructions to highlight key points and the players will then focus on these points;
- don't use jargon or over-elaborate as this will only confuse the players;
- be creative with certain phrases to emphasise key coaching points so that players remember them, e.g. 'Z' move to describe the movement of a player to create space or 'relax and find the pass' to emphasise time and being confident on the ball.

When providing feedback, describe how the session topic went, but let the players gather together as a group and reflect on their own personal performances. Sometimes you may decide that you are simply going to move on to the next part of the session and you may have a question and answer time at the end of training to highlight the key elements of the practice in one go. Whenever providing feedback, remember to be positive and give comments that they can later act on, e.g. 'can you do this next time . . . .?' rather than 'you did this so . . .!!!'. Finally, make sure the feedback is tailored to the individual or the team as a whole, unless there was a common issue throughout the players.

When you are delivering your coaching session, there are a number of coaching styles and techniques that you can use. Below are of the most common types.

- **Command** This style is effective with players of a younger age or where you are dealing with a large group of players. It makes effective use of limited time and allows you to guide players towards a level of understanding that you have set. A good example would be where you need to demonstrate to the whole group and you want their attention; the instruction of 'STOP, STAND STILL' tells them exactly what you require them to do.
- **Guided discovery** This style encourages more involvement from the player in their learning by setting them problems to solve and encouraging them to ask more questions to resolve the problems. It is good for one to one coaching, game-related practices and with more experienced players.
- **Homework** As its names suggest, this is a style of coaching that involves the players taking home some coaching points and practising alone, for example dribbling or turning skills.
- **Testing** This style involves setting the players challenges to test them and then assessing how well they do, for example running with the ball over a set distance or course in a certain time; players improvements can then be monitored as they decrease the time they need to meet the challenge.
- **Inclusive** With this style, as a coach you are looking to involve everybody in the group, regardless of ability. A warm-up/cool-down is one example of this but, in terms of training, this might be simple technical drills where everyone is picking up the techniques.
- **Practice style** The focus, here, is on practising a specific skill or range of skills and the coach will work with each player to ensure they have full understanding. Once this is achieved, the coach will then progress the group as a whole.
- **Question and answer** The skilful use of questions is becoming a more and more important tool for good coaches and can be used in conjunction with any of the styles above. It is also an excellent way of making the players feel more

involved. Be careful to use questions that need an explanation in the answer and not simply a yes or no. Also, by asking questions you will encourage the players to ask questions back to confirm understanding, to analyse their own performance and to understand the key learning factors.

The overall aim of using any of these coaching styles is to develop thinking players who will practise away from you, the football coach. Remember, good coaching may involve saying nothing if the players are already in an effective learning environment.

Briefings and de-briefings

Another useful tool to help set out the structure of your session and ensure that players fully understand what you are trying to achieve in the practice is a 'micro' briefing. If, for example, you are about to go into a technical practice on shooting, first, set up a mini version of the session to the side of the area you have organised. Tell the players who are involved in the practice where they are to stand, for example the servers, the goalkeeper, the players who will be coached on shooting and maybe an additional defender or two who may be called in as the session progresses. Using a ball, get the players to throw it to each other to simulate how the practice flows. Once the keeper has the ball, explain what he does with a save or, if the shooter scores or the ball goes wide and, finally, explain how you will progress the drill or swap players around. Once all the players understand, send them out on to your organised area.

This micro brief should last no more than two to three minutes, but it will save valuable coaching time through not having to explain to players where to stand over a much larger area or when you swap the players around.

Another example might be a phase of play on a defending topic. Set the scene for the drill. Make the attacking team the opposition for next week and explain their style of play to the players, or make them a professional team who have well-known traits (e.g. the attacking team: you are Barcelona, you are very offensive-minded and attack with speed and directness – go and do this for me). Next you may impose some conditions, i.e. 'if one attacking fullback joins the attack, the other must stay' or 'defenders, I want you to hold a high defensive line in to the midfield third' and, finally, you can explain how the area is set up, if you have target players, how the ball should be delivered to them, if you have target goals, how the ball can be played in to them etc. Finally, again get the players to throw the ball to each other to simulate how the session should run; start with the servers, explain how you want the attackers to play and then finally explain to the defenders what the session topic is and how they should play the ball out. Avoid starting on your coaching points; the idea of the briefing is to explain the topic and how the session should run.

Again, this will save you considerable time and also ensure you have a good structure to the practice which means you can get all your key coaching points out.

Once you have run your practice session, bring the players back into your briefing area and take up their final positions, but now carry out the micro de-brief. Get the players to talk you through what they did. For a technical session, get the last two players you coached to explain a couple of the key coaching points, then ask the other players to point out the other key coaching points. Maybe you throw the ball to a player and they have to give a coaching point, or have a bib to hand and use this. For a functional practice, small-sided game or phase of play, get the players to talk you through specific groups of moves, i.e. the attackers on the left, how did they progress? What happened when the defenders won the ball? How did they play? What did the right-sided players do when the ball was on the left? What communication did the keeper give? Go through all the different coaching topics you covered and ensure that each player involved answers questions on What they did and more importantly why. This will ensure all players fully under-stand what happened in the session.

Delivering the coaching session

All coaches have a different style and approach to coaching and no one way is better than another as long as each observes some core coaching qualities. Coaches should have an enthusiastic manner and display high standards of ethical behaviour, ensuring that their work is inclusive and that they encourage everyone to enjoy their football. They should be both persistent and patient and should be confident in their approach, showing the courage of their convictions. They should always display the highest levels of good practice and standards and be understanding and responsive to the needs of their players and to football in general. They should always be looking to update and grow their knowledge and understanding of the game and be open to new ideas and techniques. They need to understand how players learn and develop and how they can bring out the best in their players by setting them challenging tasks within their sessions. They should be passionate about the game and pass on this passion to others, they should also look to involve their players in the decision-making process and the learning experience by using their communication skills and influence to demonstrate achievement and development. Finally, coaches should be able to adapt, look for innovative ways to deliver their vision and knowledge, and make the learning experience fun, rewarding and enjoyable for everyone.

As you coach your team, it is important to consider your position in delivering the session. In all cases you should place yourself where you can see 'the bigger picture'. This could be to the side of the session to allow you to fully observe the whole area. If it is a defensive topic, it could be behind the goal, or level with the back four to check for positioning. For attackers, you might be on the halfway line so you can see their movement across the pitch. In fact it can be anywhere that gives you a good view of the session, where you are not interfering with play and where you can instantly be heard and be on hand to assist players. Once the session is underway, try not to ball watch but instead look at the players you are coaching. Only ever coach one team or set of players at a time but ensure you are giving positive encouragement to the other team or players on things they do well. Manage them to ensure there is realism to the practice and that the structure is kept. If there are tactical or structural factors to be addressed, stop the play and give your demonstration; if it is a technical issue in a non-technical drill, then use questions and answers to address the factor. Ensure you stick to the topic you are coaching and do not wander into other areas, as this will only confuse the players and dilute the learning process.

To deliver your coaching points, you should follow the coaching formula. Ensure you organise the session with realism in mind, make the area the correct size for the age group and topic you are coaching; if it is too small, players will be on top of each other and will rush; if it is too large, players will have too much time and space and it will be unrealistic. Ensure you get the structure of the session right to make sure you can deliver the session correctly and then let the players have a couple of phases to check that you are happy with the organisation and structure. If you are not, don't be afraid to stop and change it; better to do this a few minutes in to the session than run all the way through unrealistically. Let the players play and get some flow into the session; too much stopping and starting will tune the players out. When you see a point that needs coaching, immediately stop the play with a strong, loud command of 'STOP, STAND STILL' making sure that all players stop and go back to the position they were in when you made the call. Use one of the coaching styles above to deliver your coaching point or points and use Q&A to get your point across. Demonstrate the point, reconstruct what happened with half-paced play and then demonstrate what you want to happen. Make the players then rehearse the coaching point. If they did not rehearse it properly, show them again. Once they have rehearsed it properly, then 'play'. Observe again to make sure you are happy with that point and then move on to the next coaching point that presents itself. Do not look to force points to happen or look for mistakes, instead try and look out for the topic objectives and help your players to achieve them – work to the 'bigger picture'.

Summary of coaching formula

1 Organise realistically.
2 Set the structure for the session topic.
3 Let it run through a couple of times to make sure you are happy with points 1 and 2.

4 Let the session flow and the players play.

5 When you see a coaching point use 'STOP, STAND STILL' and recreate what happened.

6 Demonstrate how you would like it to happen.

7 Use Q&A to test for understanding.

8 Let the players rehearse the coaching point to confirm understanding, if they do not understand, demonstrate again.

9 Once they understand, let them play.

10 Re-observe performance, look for other key coaching points to deliver.

11 Don't force the points, coach what you see and work within the 'bigger picture'.

Self-evaluation and analysis

Having carried out the match analysis, preparation, planning and then delivering your sessions, it is common to simply move on to the next series of sessions and spend little time evaluating those you have delivered. This means that coaches miss an ideal opportunity to review their own performance and, if necessary, build and improve on it to become a more effective coach.

If you are an inexperienced coach, it may be difficult to take a step back and objectively look at what you have delivered and assess its merits, whether it was done in a safe coaching environment, or what modifications you could make to improve it?

Spending a short amount of time after each session to reflect on what just happened will not only help you to grow as a coach, but it will also allow you to objectively assess whether the session was a success. Can you move on to the next part of your coaching framework/monthly session planner? Or do you need to modify the session so that you can re-deliver it in an effective manner? If the session didn't meet your requirements, you may decide to postpone re-delivering it for several weeks so the players don't become bored or negative when you re-deliver it.

Finally, if you are honest in your evaluations and you are not happy with a session and feel you need to re-deliver it, feed back to your team about your evaluation and how you intend to re-deliver the session in a better way – involving them will make them feel included and should help you reach your goals.

Below is a sample of a coach's self-evaluation, followed by a template for your own use. Take some time to think about each question and then jot down your thoughts in the space provided. Be honest with yourself and try to be objective. If something was out of your control, then move on and don't dwell on it, but if you can improve, note it down and work on it in future sessions.

Session topic:	Dealing with the back pass and distribution	Session date:	30.09.10
Were there any health and safety issues that arose before, during or after the session?	Had to clear loose debris from the playing fields, I need to mention this to our club secretary and ask him to speak to the local council. Otherwise, nothing.		
Was the set-up and organisation of the area correct to meet the needs of the session? Did you have all of the necessary equipment required? Could you have improved it?	Had to work with half of a pitch due to other teams from the club training on the same pitch, ideally would have liked two-thirds of the pitch. All necessary equipment was available.		
Did the planned content of the session deliver what you required and was it understood by the players? If not, how can you improve it next time you deliver the session?	Worked primarily with the goalkeeper and back four to set their shape and structure and they understood the coaching points well. Need to ensure I revisit the session to work on the midfield and strikers as well.		
How was your coaching style and communication when delivering the session? Could it be improved upon next time?	Took up a coaching position primarily around the position of the back four to the side of the pitch. This worked well.		
Did you have to make any changes after you planned the session, but prior to delivering it or during the session? Why?	Had to reduce the length of the training area due to the reasons above and I was short of two players due to illness and injury, so I removed a server and one none-coached midfielder.		
Did the players understand and enjoy the session? Did their performance improve as you expected? If not, why not?	All of the players enjoyed the session. I tried to let it flow so they played football, but also I got out all my coaching points. The keeper and back four worked well and understood and therefore improved in this area.		
What feedback have you had from the players involved or other coaching colleagues?	My assistant coach thought the session was good, they fed back that I should maybe bring in my coaching points earlier to allow more free play at the end.		
If you were to coach this session again, how could you further improve it?	Take on board the point above, try and extend the playing area and bring in the up-field players to ensure the whole team work on the coaching points.		

Additional notes:

Progress to next session on the monthly coaching plan, but look to revisit the session before we move on to the next topic to ensure I work with the up-field players and achieve full team understanding.

Fig. 03:01 Coaching session review and self-evaluation

Session topic:		Session date:	
Were there any health and safety issues that arose before, during or after the session?			
Was the set-up and organisation of the area correct to meet the needs of the session? Did you have all of the necessary equipment required? Could you have improved upon it?			
Did the planned content of the session deliver what you required and was it understood by the players? If not, how can you improve it next time you deliver the session?			
How was your coaching style and communication when delivering the session? Could it be improved upon next time?			
Did you have to make any changes after you planned the session, but prior to delivering it or during the session? Why?			
Did the players understand and enjoy the session? Did their performance improve as you expected? If not, why not?			
What feedback have you had from the players involved or other coaching colleagues?			
If you were to coach this session again, how could you further improve it?			
Additional notes:			

Coaching session review and self-evalution template

Player development

For your players to understand their own competencies and abilities, the areas they need to work on and the goals you would like them to aspire to, you need to provide them with some analytical feedback which they can absorb, question and respond to. An ideal way to do this is to carry out mid-season and end of season reviews. The end of season review can also be used to monitor progress at the beginning of the following season and to see if the players have been thinking about and, better still, working on in the close season.

Provided here is a template for conducting a review for both the goalkeeper and outfield players and it can be used at both the mid-season and end of season. It initially focuses on the player's technical ability generally and then hones in on specific technical aspects of their ability. The form then looks at their insight into games, their personality and finally their physical make-up.

It is up to you as a coach to decide how you mark the form but, as a rule of thumb, an average member of the squad would score 'B' for the core skills. Therefore look at your squad as a whole and pick a player who sits in the middle of the squad for each section, i.e. 'technical', 'insight', 'personality' and 'speed/athleticism' and then mark the rest of your squad around these averages. It may be that one player can be used for all the groups, or you may set your average mark around two, three or four players, one for each section.

The coach's comments allow you to highlight areas that you feel the player has done well in and other areas where you feel they need to concentrate on to take them to the next level. These may be technical, insight or personality, but this is your opportunity to highlight these key points and get your message across to both the player and their parents/guardians.

The second page allows the player and the parent to give their feedback on the report. Try and get them to be as constructive as possible and not simply put 'I agree/disagree'. Ask them to highlight their own personal achievements and their own thoughts on how they could develop and ask the parents/guardians for feedback on how they feel the team is being run and the level of coaching etc.

Finally, the third box allows you, the parents/guardians and the player to set goals. Look to set at least three objectives and ideally a maximum of five (more than this will give them too much to think about and the focus will be lost). These goals then form the basis for the next review and also allow you to monitor a player's progression.

See the following example of a review form, and a template so that you can prepare your own.

Name:	Jamie Fisher
Date:	28th December
Position:	Midfield

Fig. 03:02 Player assessment feedback form – outfield player

Technical	Base	C	B-	B	B+	A
Receiving	Ability to cushion the ball			✓		
Receiving	First touch under pressure			✓		
Passing	Accuracy – short				✓	
Passing	Both feet				✓	
Shooting	Accuracy				✓	
Heading	Technique			✓		
Attacking	1 v 1 Attacking			✓		
Defending	1 v 1 Defending			✓		
Technical	Base	C	B-	B	B+	A
Receiving	First touch creates space			✓		
Passing	Accuracy – long				✓	
Passing	Penetration				✓	
Shooting	Power				✓	
Shooting	Takes responsibility				✓	
Heading	Attitude			✓		
Attacking	Speed and penetration			✓		
Attacking	Use of fakes and turns			✓		
Insight		C	B-	B	B+	A
Decision-making	On the ball				✓	
Anticipation	Reading the game				✓	
Game play	Positional awareness				✓	
Game play	Affects the game				✓	
Personality		C	B-	B	B+	A
Enthusiasm				✓		
Motivated to improve				✓		
Focus in training				✓		
Communication				✓		
Speed/athleticism		C	B-	B	B+	A
Speed			✓			
Strength					✓	
Agility				✓		
Coordination				✓		
		C	B-	B	B+	A
	Technical				✓	
	Insight				✓	
	Personality			✓		
	Speed/athleticism			✓		
	Overall grade			✓		

Coach's comments:

Jamie is an integral member of the team and has made one of the central midfield positions his own. However, to further improve his game, Jamie needs to work on playing with his head up to see all the options open to him, be more prepared to take players on in midfield and look to release the ball more quickly on occasion. Sometimes he takes a touch too many and puts himself under pressure.

Name: Simon Jay
Signed:
Date: 28/12/2010

Player's comments:

I agree in general with Simon's comments, but do feel that I do make an effort to take on players 1 v 1. I will work on playing with my head up more and I also think this will help me see more quickly the passes I could make. I enjoy training with the squad and will continue to work hard in training to improve my game.

Name: Jamie Fisher
Signed:
Date: 28/12/2010

Parents' comments:

We agree with both Simon and Jamie's comments and have seen a great improvement in Jamie's overall ability. He enjoys being part of the team and looks forward to training and games. Our only comment on the team is that one or two players seem to mess about a bit in training and cause some of the other players to lose focus.

Name: Mr and Mrs Fisher
Signed:
Date: 28/12/2010

Player's objectives:

- Concentrate on playing with your head up, especially in matches to see the bigger picture.
- Work on releasing the ball quickly in training so that this improves within games
- Watch some live games and the players that play in your position and look at their decision-making and when they keep the ball, release the ball or attack players 1 v 1.

Player's signature: .... Date: ....
Parent's signature: .... Date: ....
Manager's signature: .... Date: ....
Coach's signature: .... Date: ....

Player assessment feedback form – outfield player (template)

Name:	
Date:	
Position:	

Technical	Base	C	B-	B	B+	A
Receiving	Ability to cushion the ball					
Receiving	First touch under pressure					
Passing	Accuracy – short					
Passing	Both feet					
Shooting	Accuracy					
Heading	Technique					
Attacking	1 v 1 Attacking					
Defending	1 v 1 Defending					
Technical	Base	C	B-	B	B+	A
Receiving	First touch creates space					
Passing	Accuracy – long					
Passing	Penetration					
Shooting	Power					
Shooting	Takes responsibility					
Heading	Attitude					
Attacking	Speed and penetration					
Attacking	Use of fakes and turns					
Insight		C	B-	B	B+	A
Decision-making	On the ball					
Anticipation	Reading the game					
Game play	Positional awareness					
Game play	Affects the game					
Personality		C	B-	B	B+	A
Enthusiasm						
Motivated to improve						
Focus in training						
Communication						
Speed/athleticism		C	B-	B	B+	A
Speed						
Strength						
Agility						
Coordination						
		C	B-	B	B+	A
	Technical					
	Insight					
	Personality					
	Speed/athleticism					
	Overall grade					

Coach's comments:

Name:
Signed:
Date:

Player's comments:

Name:
Signed:
Date:

Parents' comments:

Name:
Signed:
Date:

Player's objectives:

Player's signature: .... Date: ....
Parent's signature: .... Date: ....
Manager's signature: .... Date: ....
Coach's signature: .... Date: ....

Player assessment feedback form–goalkeeper (template)

Name:	
Date:	
Position:	Goalkeeper

Technical	Base	C	B-	B	B+	A
Receiving	Ability to cushion the ball			✓		
Receiving	First touch under pressure			✓		
Passing	Accuracy – short				✓	
Passing	Both feet				✓	
Shooting	Accuracy				✓	
Heading	Technique			✓		
Attacking	1 v 1 Attacking			✓		
Defending	1 v 1 Defending			✓		
Technical	Base	C	B-	B	B+	A
Receiving	First touch creates space			✓		
Passing	Accuracy – long				✓	
Passing	Penetration				✓	
Shooting	Power				✓	
Shooting	Takes responsibility				✓	
Heading	Attitude			✓		
Attacking	Speed and penetration			✓		
Attacking	Use of fakes and turns			✓		
Insight		C	B-	B	B+	A
Decision-making	On the ball				✓	
Anticipation	Reading the game				✓	
Game play	Positional awareness				✓	
Game play	Affects the game				✓	
Personality		C	B-	B	B+	A
Enthusiasm				✓		
Motivated to improve				✓		
Focus in training				✓		
Communication				✓		
Speed/athleticism		C	B-	B	B+	A
Speed			✓			
Strength					✓	
Agility				✓		
Coordination				✓		
		C	B-	B	B+	A
	Technical			✓		
	Insight				✓	
	Personality			✓		
	Speed/athleticism			✓		
	Overall grade			✓		

Coach's comments:

Name:
Signed:
Date:

Player's comments:

Name:
Signed:
Date:

Parents' comments:

Name:
Signed:
Date:

Player's objectives:

Player's signature: ....   Date: ....
Parent's signature: ....   Date: ....
Manager's signature: ....   Date: ....
Coach's signature: ....   Date: ....

part two
coaching
sessions

04
Practice type definitions

Now that the match analysis has been carried out and evaluated, the long-term coaching framework has been planned and the monthly session planners have been formulated, it is time to start delivering the coaching sessions. Different types of coaching practices have been mentioned and a more detailed explanation of each type of session is given below, including the benefits that each session offers, when to use them, guidelines on how long each session should last, how to set up and structure each type of session, along with a key to the symbols used.

Technical practice

A technical practice works on the technique of the individual player in an unopposed environment. Work on a specific game-related skill and introduce each coaching point in a logical sequence. Challenge technique by increasing or decreasing the size of the practice area, the time allowed, or the difficulty of the practice. Progress the practice as the individual improves to further challenge technique.

For a technical practice, the size of the area to work in should be realistic for the age and ability of the players involved. Set up the coaching area and cone it off to clearly identify the area. As the players technically improve you can increase or decrease the size of the area accordingly. If you have planned for progressions in the session then, where possible, mark these out in advance.

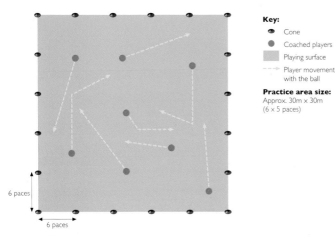

Key:
- ◐ Cone
- ● Coached players
- ▨ Playing surface
- ---▸ Player movement with the ball

Practice area size:
Approx. 30m x 30m
(6 x 5 paces)

6 paces

6 paces

Fig. 04:01 Technical practice area of play

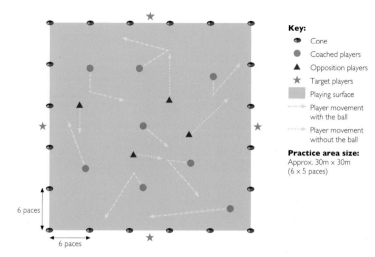

Key:
◉ Cone
● Coached players
▲ Opposition players
★ Target players
▨ Playing surface
- - -➤ Player movement with the ball
······➤ Player movement without the ball

Practice area size:
Approx. 30m x 30m
(6 x 5 paces)

Fig. 04:02 Skill practice area of play

Skill practice

A skill practice is an opposed practice that works on the dual development of improving technique and decision-making. All players will have individual objectives for the practice, which will be based on the theme of the practice. The size and number of players involved will vary depending on the theme of the session and the practice may contain imposed conditions to enhance training.

For a skill practice, the size of the area to work in should be realistic for the age and ability of the players involved (see Fig. 04:02). Set up the coaching area and cone it off to clearly identify the area; as the players technically improve you can increase or decrease the size of the area accordingly. If you have planned for progressions in the session then, where possible, mark these out in advance.

Fig. 04:02 would be a logical progression from the technical practice of running with the ball. By introducing defenders into the practice, the players not only have to work on the technical aspects of running with the ball, but they now have to work on their decision-making regarding where to run, how and when to shield the ball, deciding on what type of touch they should use, and should they run with the ball, or turn/dribble.

Functional practice

A functional practice is also an opposed practice that works on either an individual or small group of players in a specific part of the pitch, to develop an understanding of their specific roles, responsibilities and skills for a particular role. This could be an attacking role or a defensive role.

For a functional practice, the size of the area to work in should be realistic for the

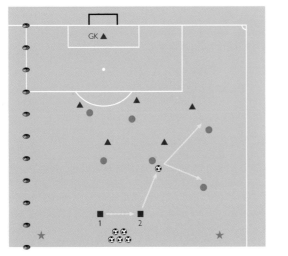

Key:

⬮ Cone
⊙ Ball
● Coached players
▲ Opposition players
★ Target players
■ Servers
▨ Playing surface
— Pass of the ball

Practice area size:
• Relevant to theme being practiced
• Mark out area with cones 6 paces apart

Fig. 04:03 Functional practice area of play

age and ability of the players involved. Set up the coaching area on the part of the pitch that is specific to the theme being worked on and cone it off to clearly identify the area (allow for the fact that this can be changed as the practice progresses and you introduce further players).

The example in Fig. 04:03 would use the skills acquired in the 'running with the ball' practices, but now it is being used within a function working on the play of a wide midfielder and attacking fullback. The coach is working with the blue players to improve the attacking capabilities on the right flank with the aim of increasing the number of crosses made into the penalty area. A natural progression would then be to work on the finishing skills of the two strikers and shape of the two attacking midfielders. To give the defending team some objectives, if they win the ball, can they play it to the target players with control? Functional practices should be planned to meet the theme you want to address and the players you want to involve and then match them with the correct amount of defenders. Work on this theme in the functional practice and then watch the players in a game to assess their understanding.

Phase of play

A phase of play is a practice situation that utilises the full width of the pitch but with a reduced length. It involves two teams, one attacking and one defending as is used to develop team, group or unit understanding. The coach will work with one team and focus on either an attacking or defending theme, looking to develop understanding of patterns of play and tactical understanding.

For a phase of play, as stated, work with the full width of the pitch, but ensure the

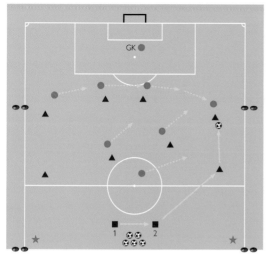

Key:
- 🌢 Cone
- ☺ Ball
- ● Coached players
- ▲ Opposition players
- ★ Target players
- ■ Servers
- ▨ Playing surface
- ┄┄▸ Player movement without the ball
- ──▸ Pass of the ball

Practice area size:
- Full width of pitch
- Length to suit topic

Fig. 04:04 Phase of play practice area

depth of the pitch allows you to coach your topic. Clearly mark the thirds of the pitch so that the players can see where they are within the pitch and allow the game to flow enough to create realistic situations. Ensure all players take up realistic positions at the start of the practice. Each time you reset the practice, make sure you give objectives for both sets of players so you can create realistic scenarios. Finally ensure the servers play the ball in, to again provide realism.

The example in Fig. 04:04 would work on the defensive shape of the blue team. Set the red team the task of attacking quickly, working the ball wide to put the defending fullbacks under pressure. The coach would look to work with the three separate units - the 'back four' and their decision-making based on the actions of the nearest defender, in this case the left fullback, the two midfield players and finally the retreating striker. Let the play flow initially to see the patterns of play.

Small-sided games

A small-sided game is a practice played with two teams, each with a goalkeeper, and the size of the sides is less than 11 v 11. The practice can be used by the coach to work on technical or tactical themes and is perfect for developing the principles of game play and team understanding. The coach should normally work with one team and on one specific theme.

The area and goals should be adapted to suit the age and ability of the players. It should use official game rules, but not include corners. Ensure that the thirds of the pitch are clearly marked so that players know what zone they are in, and also ensure balls are adequately placed around the pitch to keep the practice moving. Both teams need

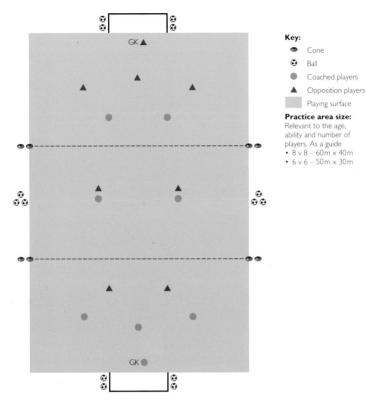

Key:

- Cone
- Ball
- Coached players
- ▲ Opposition players
- Playing surface

Practice area size:
Relevant to the age, ability and number of players. As a guide
- 8 v 8 – 60m x 40m
- 6 v 6 – 50m x 30m

Fig. 04:05 Small-sided games practice area of play

different coloured bibs, but the keepers do not wear bibs. Finally, at the beginning of the practice, after a goal is scored, or whenever you want to bring structure back to the session get both teams to 'set-up' in the 'structured start' position (see Fig. 04:05 above). There are several variations to the small-sided game, depending on what topic it is that you are coaching. Where you stand and which team starts with the ball will change, e.g. when coaching an attacking topic, possession should start with midfield players from the team you are not coaching; for a defending topic, start possession with the team you are coaching. To start, the midfield player should take a touch out of his feet and then pass to either of their forward teammates.

Warm-ups and cool-downs

At the beginning of any practice session and prior to a game it is vital that the players undergo a thorough warm-up to prepare them, both physically and mentally, for the forthcoming physical activity, and to ensure that they can perform at an optimum level. A warm-up does not need to be bland and boring; it can contain a wide degree of variety to keep the players interested and get them 'tuned-in' for the session or game to come.

A thorough warm-up will:
- help to raise muscle temperature;
- increase the blood flow through the muscles;
- stretch the muscles and increase the joint mobility;
- gradually prepare the cardiovascular and respiratory systems, building them up to full performance and not overloading them, which can actually cause a loss of performance;
- prepare the players mentally, allowing them to 'tune-in' for the forthcoming exercise.

Ideally, a warm-up should constitute three specific phases. The first warm-up phase gets the blood circulating and the respiratory system pumping oxygen to the muscles to give them the energy to work. This warm-up phase raises the body temperature and starts to loosen up the different muscle groups.

The second phase involves stretching the major muscles groups and flexing the joints of the body. In times gone by this stretching would consist mainly of static stretching, e.g. a group of players in a circle with legs shoulder-width apart bending at the waist to stretch a muscle group. This should be avoided as you are allowing your body temperature to cool down, and when a muscle is stretched when not fully warmed up, it can take up to an hour to fully recover its strength and elasticity. Ideally your stretching should be in the form of dynamic stretches, which consist of functional-based exercises that use sport-specific movements to prepare the body for activity. Dynamic stretching consists of controlled leg and arm swings that take you (gently!) to the limits of your range of motion without bouncing or jerking movements.

Finally, the third phase of a warm-up uses specific exercises and drills to prepare the players for the exercise to come. It should be performed at a high tempo to ensure that the players are 'match' ready. How often have you heard the comment that the team didn't get in to the game until after the first 15 minutes of the match? This is usually due to a lack of proper warm-up, and this final phase should end with an exercise that is at full match tempo.

Make sure that any warm-up is prepared and timed properly. A warm-up should last between 10 and 30 minutes and should not be completed too early, as the effects will dissipate after 20–30 minutes of inactivity.

Try to introduce a ball at the start of phase one, which will allow the players to get psychologically prepared and the whole warm-up phase to be football specific. Try to create a standard routine – your players will become familiar enough with it so that they are able to carry out the warm-up themselves, leaving you time to prepare the area for the coming session. Alternatively, you can vary the warm-up each time to keep it fresh and engaging.

Give the following selection of sample warm-ups a try and work out what you like best as a routine or keep mixing them up to vary your warm-ups.

Sample warm-ups

Set up an area 30m x 30m, each player has a ball.

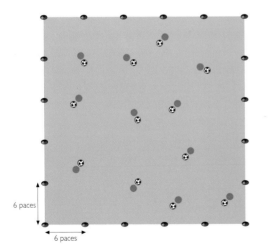

6 paces

6 paces

Fig. 05:01 Warm-up set-up

Pairs – 100 touches

Each player jogs around with the ball and takes 100 touches with the inside and outside of their feet (don't allow them to pass or juggle the ball from foot to foot). Performing 100 touches raises the heart rate and starts the blood pumping.

Fig. 05:02 Warm-up 100 touches

Fig. 05:03 Bouncing the ball off the thigh

Bouncing the ball off the thigh

Carry on jogging, but now bounce the ball off a thigh and catch it, jog some more and then bounce it off the other thigh. This action starts to stretch the quads and hamstrings.

Fig. 05:04 Throwing the ball and catching high

Throwing and catching high

Carry on jogging and now throw the ball into the air and catch it high. Ensure that they catch it with straight arms to stretch their sides. This stretches the arms and sides (latissimus dorsi muscles).

Flicking the ball

Players group into pairs, a ball per pair. One player holds the ball in front of him at head height and the second player tries to flick the back of the ball. If they can reach without stretching, hold the ball higher. Do five on each foot and then swap. This will stretch the calf muscles and hamstrings.

Fig. 05:05 Flicking the ball

Side foot-volleys

One player throws the ball to the side of his partner at waist height and the partner side foot-volleys the ball back. Do five on each side and then swap. This will stretch the groin muscles.

Fig. 05:06 Side foot-volleys

Knee tennis

Players now lunge and knee the ball between each other (knee tennis). Each player performs a minimum of five lunges on each knee. The groin muscles will be stretched even further, as will the large leg muscle groups.

Over and above this, you could also include a jumping and heading practice,

Fig. 05:07 Knee tennis

chesting or any other exercise to work football specific themes. You will have fulfilled both phase one and phase two of the warm-up and you can now progress to phase three and begin an intensive warm-up.

Warm-up one

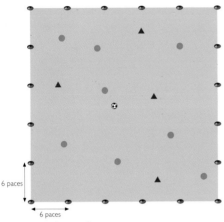

6 paces

6 paces

Fig. 05:08 Intensive warm-up one

Play overloaded defenders against attackers. The blue players have to keep possession for a set number of passes. If the defenders win the ball, the blue players can undertake a forfeit (sprint around the playing area, ten press-ups/sit-ups etc). Keep changing the defenders regularly and allow brief breaks to take fluid on board.

Warm-up two

Get the players in a circle again with overloaded attackers against defenders. There are a number of ways to work this warm-up: request a minimum two-touch to work on control and pass selection; a pass and follow, with the pass being played to at least a player one removed from the player with the ball; or one-touch to work on speed of play and the defenders' effort. Swap the defenders regularly.

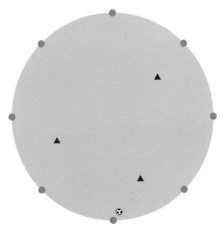

Fig. 05:09 Intensive warm-up two

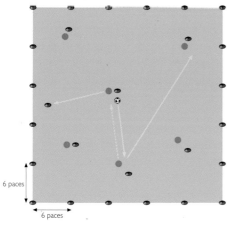

Fig. 05:10 Intensive warm-up three

Warm-up three

Set cones up to be well apart in your 30m x 30m square. Include one player less than the number of cones, i.e. eight cones, seven players. Players pass the ball with a good weight to make the receiving player work on his controlling touch. The passing player then sprints to the spare cone, and the player who controlled the pass now becomes the passing player and he sprints to the spare cone. Make the players work for a maximum of five minutes and then give them a break.

Warm-up four

Shadow play. Get the players in pairs, one with a ball, one without. Place them either side of two cones spaced 5m apart. The player with the ball makes turns and feints between the cones, and his partner shadows his moves. Swap players regularly.

Fig. 05:11 Intensive warm-up four

Cool-down

As with a warm-up, a thorough cool-down following any match or training session is essential, but many players and coaches still often overlook it. The aim of a cool-down is to allow the body to gradually make the transition from full exercise mode to a non-exercise state, therefore avoiding injury, stiffness and muscle tiredness the following day.

There are many benefits of an effective cool-down. An effective cool-down assists the removal of waste products that accumulate in the muscles during rigorous exercise, such as lactic acid. It gradually decreases the body temperature, heart rate and blood pressure, and releases hormones that counter the effects of adrenaline, which can make you feel restless after strenuous exercise. Finally, by stretching immediately after a football match the muscles are still warm and can therefore be manipulated more easily, thereby increasing flexibility.

The most beneficial result of an efficient cool-down is the player's improved recovery time. In the modern game, footballers are increasingly called upon to play two or even three games a week and a proper cool-down is therefore essential. Getting the players used to the ritual of a proper cool-down from an early age will only stand them in good stead through their playing careers – in recent years, the cool-down has become increasingly pivotal in the match and training regimes of professional football clubs. Don't let the weather prevent you from performing an effective cool-down, as the stretching components can be completed inside the dressing room or a hall or gym if one is available.

Procedure

A cool-down over a period of 5–10 minutes is generally considered adequate and essentially involves gradually decreasing the intensity of the exercise. Start with a slow jog with gradual reductions to a brisk walk, with muscle stretching exercises incorporated at intervals on, for example, each corner of half of the pitch. Slowly reducing exercise intensity in this way helps to lower the heart rate gradually, avoiding a sudden stop in strenuous activity that can actually force the heart to work harder initially. A gradual decline in heart rate reduces the stress placed on the heart.

Following the jog, various muscle groups must be stretched. In this instance, use static stretches to work the muscles. Hold each stretch for 12–15 seconds without bouncing and repeat three times. As well as traditional stretching exercises, it is also advisable to perform around five minutes of callisthenic-type exercises, such as alternate toe touches with your legs apart or lying on your back and cycling your legs in the air. Finally, finish the cool-down with two minutes of jogging at a slow pace, while kicking and shaking the arms and legs loose.

A range of static stretches
Touch your toes

- Stand with feet shoulder-width apart, legs locked.
- Bend down to try to touch your toes.
- You should feel the strech all the way up the backs of your legs.

Quadriceps stretch
- Balance on one leg pulling the foot of the other leg into the rear.
- You should feel a stretch across the front of the thigh muscle (quadriceps).
- Swap legs and repeat the process.

Calf stretch
- Get into a press-up position, one foot behind the other, and push your rear into the air. Then try to push the heel of your foot on the floor towards the ground.
- You should feel a stretch in your calf muscle.
- Swap legs and repeat the process.

Hamstring stretch
- Stand upright with one leg behind the other. With legs locked, bend down and touch your toes.
- To stretch further, try to lift your toes upwards.
- You should feel a stretch across the back of your thigh muscle (hamstring).

Adductor stretch

- Sit on your rear and bring the soles of your feet together in front of you.
- Place your elbows on the inside of your knees and press your legs downwards.
- You should feel a stretch across your inner thigh muscles (adductors).

Lunges

- Step forward, bending at the knee.
- Do not allow your knee to go past the line of your toes.
- Lunge alternately left and right, five times on each leg.

A range of callisthenic stretches

Shoulder stretch

- Stand with legs shoulder-width apart.
- Alternately touch each big toe with the opposite hand.

Cycling

- Lie on your back and cycle your legs in the air.
- Try doing it backwards as well.

Standing cycling

- With one leg locked, cycle the other leg in a slow forward rotation.
- Ensure the toes of that leg stay pointed upright through the whole leg rotation.

Lower to sitting position

- Standing upright with feet together bend your legs together and slowly lower yourself down to just above a sitting position and then lift slowly to upright.
- Repeat 10 times.

Sample session plans

The following are sample session plans that will cover the principles and techniques of goalkeeping, defending and attacking.

Goalkeeping
This chapter will illustrate session plans covering goalkeeping technique, shot-stopping, narrowing the angle, dealing with crosses, distribution and dealing with back passes.

Principles of defending
This chapter will illustrate session plans covering basic defending principles of 1 v 1, 2 v 2, 4 v 4, and as a unit. It will then progress to defending when organised, defending when outnumbered, roles and responsibilities in different areas of the field, tracking runners, cover and balance, and defensive heading.

Principles of attacking
This chapter will illustrate session plans covering basic attacking principles of 1 v 1, 2 v 2, 4 v 4, and as a unit. It will then progress to creating space, support play, development of possession, counter-attacking, running with the ball, wide play, dribbling, turning, shooting, one-touch play, and attacking heading.

Attacking and defending set pieces
This chapter will illustrate session plans covering basic attacking and defending principles of set pieces to include corners, free kicks and throw-ins. Defensively, it will look at zonal marking, man for man marking and a combination of both.

All of the session plans will include an explanation of the set-up, i.e. is it a functional practice or technical practice? Each will explain how the session is run, i.e. who starts the session? How is the ball played in? 'Key factors' will outline the coaching points that you should be looking for the drill to work on. A number of the sessions may seem similar but have a different theme and it is important to choose a session for the theme you are looking to work on. However, the book may not cover a particular theme to your exact requirements, so feel free to modify them to work on the exact aspects you want to cover; use the enclosed session plans as guides to build your own unique session.

Key coaching criteria and philosophies

Below are the key things that you need to think about before, during and after a practice session. Now that you are going to adopt this method of delivering your coaching sessions, why not jot down the points below and take them with you to your next few practice sessions. Make sure both your session and your coaching is addressing each of these points as you deliver your sessions. Alternatively, is there a parent or coaching colleague that can assess you?

Know the subject and theme

Once you have chosen the session plan/s you wish to deliver, make sure you read and understand the key factors for each plan with regards to both technical and tactical outcome.

Plan and prepare your strategy

By doing this you will know the positions you want your players to set up for both attacking and defending. You can then feed this information to your players in the micro-briefing session and this will mean you can spend more time coaching movement and decision-making, and less time on coaching 'out of position' mistakes and poor shape.

Fully understand the key factors for the session

- Planning and organisation

    ‣ What area of the field will you be able to use? Ensure the goal size and practice area is relevant to the age of the players.
    ‣ How many players will you have?
    ‣ Via the micro-briefing, can you ensure the practice is realistic, can you fully explain the structure you wish the players to adopt, have you explained the topic and theme properly?
    ‣ How will you start the practice – is the server playing the ball in realistically?

- Observation

    ‣ At the beginning of the practice, can you check that the organisation is correct and if not, can you adapt it?
    ‣ Are players in the correct structure/shape and if not, can you correct them?
    ‣ Do the players show the right attitude – are they tuned in for the practice?
    ‣ Can you observe the decision-making of both the individual players and the group as a whole, i.e. can you see the 'pictures' of what is happening on the field of play?

- Testing understanding

  ‣ Using one of the coaching styles explained in chapter 3, such as Question & Answer or guided discovery, can you test and check the knowledge and understanding of the players?
  ‣ Get the players to show you the coaching point and test understanding (remember, by including and involving the players in checking their knowledge, you will get a better reaction from the players).

- Coaching demonstrations

  ‣ Rather than asking a question and then explaining the answer, can you provide an example demonstration of the coaching point you want to explain? Remember the old adage a picture paints a thousand words, a good demonstration saves a thousand words.
  ‣ Once you have done this, get the players to practise a semi-live demonstration, if it doesn't work, get them to do it again!
  ‣ Get them to then do a live demonstration (make sure they practise live the point you have just coached, again don't be afraid to make them do it again if it doesn't work).
  ‣ Remember, the demonstration should be broken down into simple points, it should be clear and it should highlight the key coaching point or objective.
  ‣ A demonstration should explain to the player/s exactly what you require and it should always be positive.

- Communication

  ‣ Be loud, positive and concise.
  ‣ Get the players' interest by speaking in a positive and instructive manner.
  ‣ Avoid negativity, always be positive.
  ‣ Make sure you know your topic, players will quickly realise if you don't.
  ‣ Speak clearly and do not rush your points.
  ‣ Vary the sound and pitch of your voice to enable you to control the coaching environment, if the point is important, get that message across through the use of your voice.
  ‣ Always ask questions and provide feedback in a positive manner – don't ask 'what did you do wrong there?' but rather 'what could you have done to improve that?'
  ‣ Always ask open questions that require an answer other than yes or no. Wait for the answer and, if you need to, provide the beginning to prompt the player.

- Coaching qualities

  ‣ Always have an enthusiastic manner.
  ‣ Always dress appropriately for the coaching session, remember, if you 'look like a coach – you'll feel like a coach'.
  ‣ Display the highest levels of ethical behaviour, best practice and standards possible.
  ‣ Have the courage of your convictions – be both patient and persistent to get the best from your players.
  ‣ Challenge yourself to fully understand how your players learn and develop, include them in decision-making, understanding and the learning process.
  ‣ Be open to new ideas and learning experiences for yourself as a coach. Make sure you can adapt both within a practice session and with your own techniques and practices.
  ‣ Remember you are not only a coach, but a leader and a role model too. If you can encourage and engage your players, they will have a very positive experience and this is the most rewarding experience of all for both the players and YOU.

Key to session plans (starting overleaf)

⬮	Cone	GK ●/GK ▲	Goalkeeper
⊗	Ball	●/▲ LB	Left back
●	Coached players	●/▲ CBL	Left centre-back
C	Coach	●/▲ CBR	Right centre-back
▲	Opposition players	●/▲ RB	Right back
△	Neutral players	●/▲ LM	Left midfield
★	Target players	●/▲ CM1	Centre-midfield 1
■	Servers	●/▲ CM2	Centre-midfield 2
●	Assistant referee	●/▲ RM	Right midfield
	Playing surface	●/▲ ST1	Striker 1
- - -➤	Player movement with the ball	●/▲ ST2	Striker 2
· · · ·➤	Player movement without the ball		
⟶	Pass of the ball		
⌐‾¬	Goal		
⬮- - - - -⬮	Boundaries of practice area (distance between cones – 6 paces)		

goalkeeper

Technical practice

01. Goalkeeping basics – body stance (15–20 mins)
Set-up
Set up as a technical practice. The drill involves working on either a single goalkeeper or if two keepers are available, pair them up.

Drill flow
With a ball between two, the ball is played overarm and between the two players or the single keeper and the server.

Key factors
■ Make sure the shots are varied and between the two cones, i.e. on target.
■ The keeper must ensure that he has the correct position in the middle of the goal, between shots he needs to glance at the posts to ensure he is correctly positioned and that his position from the goal line is correct. For close-range shots, as in this session, he should be approximately 1m from the goal line.
■ In terms of stance, the keeper's feet should be shoulder-width apart and his weight should be on the balls of his feet and NOT on his heels.
■ One foot should be slightly in front of the other and, as he meets the ball, he should step into it to make his movement positive and forwards.
■ Hands should be at waist height, just in front of the body and in a position that is comfortable for the keeper.
■ His head should be still and his eyes should be looking both at the ball and the player to try and judge their intentions.
■ Most importantly, his head should be slightly forward from his body so that his weight is over his toes. Work on the saying 'nose over toes' and this will ensure the keeper has the correct stance in terms of weight distribution.
■ The keeper should have a body stance that is big, balanced and ready for quick movement.
■ Finally, his attitude should be relaxed, not too tense, but alert and ready to act immediately.

Technical practice

02. Ball handling and shot stopping (15–20 mins)

Set-up

Set up as a technical practice session. The drill involves working on either a single goalkeeper or, if two keepers are available, pair them up.

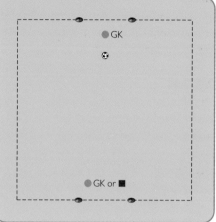

Drill

With a ball between two, played overarm between the two players or the single keeper and Server.

Key factors

- Ensure the shots are varied and between the two cones, i.e. on target.
- Ensure the keeper is alert and in the ready position with his nose over his toes.
- For shots above head height, the keeper should judge the line and flight of the ball and then attack the ball by going to meet it.
- Ensure he has the correct body action when he jumps to meet the ball. Can he lift one of his legs to offer protection for his body and can he meet the ball at its highest point?
- When catching the ball, his hands should form a 'W' shape with thumbs touching and should be firmly planted behind and in the middle of the ball.
- If the player was under pressure, he should bring the ball in and if necessary fall forwards to the ground to protect the ball and possession. If he is not under pressure can he keep the ball at arm's length and look for quick distribution options?
- For shots at chest height, can he move into the line of flight of the ball and have his hands in the 'W' position with arms half extended? Again, if pressured, bring the ball into the body, otherwise keep arms extended for quick distribution.
- For waist-height saves, can the keeper stoop down and bring his hands under and up the ball to scoop it into his chest again, going to ground if under pressure?
- Thigh-high saves require the keeper to swivel on the balls of his feet and bring his trailing leg into a 'K' leg stance to form a barrier. As with the waist-height save, scoop the ball into the chest.
- If under pressure, then rather than the 'K' leg stance, instead fall forwards in line with the flight of the ball, scooping the ball into the chest and going to ground on the forearms, protecting the ball.
- For ground saves, the keeper should move quickly into the line of the ball, swivel his leading foot and kneel to form a barrier with both legs. His hands should go down on to and behind the ball.
- If under pressure fall forwards scooping the ball into the chest, if not keep at arm's length and be ready for quick distribution. Make the barrier and scoop the ball into the chest.
- For diving saves, ensure the keeper is alert and in the ready position. For long-range shots can the keeper bring his legs together, without crossing, to move across the goal and into the flight of the ball?
- Ensure he pushes off with the foot nearest the ball and decides early if he can catch the ball cleanly, or deflect it around the post with a locked wrist and his hand.

goalkeeper

Skills practice

03. Narrowing the angle (15–20 mins)
Set-up
Set up as a skills practice. The practice involves working on the goalkeeper. The opposition is from two strikers. A server is required to feed the ball to the strikers.

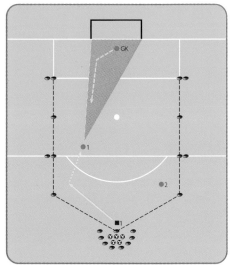

Drill flow
The ball is played from server 1 to Blue 1 and Blue 2 alternately. These attacking players then attempt to score a goal but are allowed a maximum of three touches before they can shoot. Once the ball has been played to a striker, then the keeper needs to react quickly and close down/narrow the angles.

Key factors
- Ensure the attackers are direct and initially do not attempt to go around the keeper, but after a maximum of three touches, they then shoot at goal. Once the keeper is confident on narrowing the angle, allow the strikers to be more creative.
- Ensure the keeper is alert and in the ready position with his nose over his toes and that he is correctly positioned in relation to the goal line.
- His initial movement to get into line with the striker should be with sideways steps being careful not to cross his feet, as this will put him off balance. Keep steps close to the ground for quick reaction.
- The keeper must assess if he is to advance and narrow the angle, or to set himself for a shot at goal, and be balanced and ready to make the save.
- If the keeper assesses that the striker is going to travel with the ball, i.e. he plays it out of his feet, then the keeper should advance quickly down the line of the ball.
- The keeper should move as quickly as possible, but ensure he has good balance and can get into the set or ready position as the striker shoots.
- If the striker plays the ball too far in front, and the keeper is confident he can win the ball, he should advance and collect the ball.
- If the striker shoots and the shot is near the body, the keeper should not be afraid to use his feet, his arms and hands, or just his hands to make the save.
- If the shot is away from the body, the keeper must adjust his bodyweight on to the foot nearest the ball and push off with this leg to make the dive and save.
- Once the keeper is confident, progress to allow the strikers to take as many touches as they want, to become creative in their decision-making and, if you have time, to pass between themselves.
- Look for the keeper's decision-making, be positive in your advice and remind him that goals WILL get scored.

Skills practice

04. Keeper spreading his body (15–20 mins)
Set-up

Set up as a skills practice. The practice involves working on the goalkeeper. The opposition is from two strikers. A server feeds the ball to the strikers.

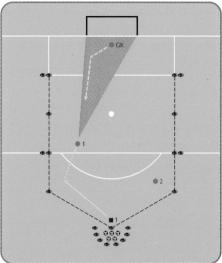

Drill flow

The ball is played from Server 1 to Blue 1 and Blue 2 alternately. These attacking players then attempt to score by shooting or rounding the keeper. Once the ball has been played to a striker, the keeper should react quickly to close down/narrow angles.

Key factors

- Ensure the keeper is alert and in the ready position, with his nose over his toes and that he is correctly positioned in relation to the goal line.
- Ensure the attackers are direct and positive towards attacking goal. After a short period, get the server to vary his passes so the keeper has to have his wits about him.
- His initial movement to get into line with the striker should be with sideways steps, being careful not to cross his feet, as this will put him off balance. Keep steps close to the ground for quick reactions.
- The keeper must assess if he is to advance and narrow the angle, or to set himself for a shot at goal, being balanced and ready to make the save.
- If the keeper assesses that the striker is going to travel with the ball, i.e. he plays it out of his feet, then the keeper should advance quickly down the line of the ball.
- The keeper should remain upright and as big as possible for as long as possible, and try and force the striker to dribble around him.
- As soon as the striker attempts to dribble around the keeper, can he go in the direction of the dribble and get his hands to the ball by diving to ground, being careful to claim the ball before he makes any contact with the player?
- If the keeper sees that the striker is going to shoot, can he assess the type of shot? If it is low, can he collapse by moving his leading leg behind his lagging leg and make a long barrier to block the shot?
- The keeper should ensure his hands are nearest to the ball to collect where possible.
- Above all, the keeper should make his decisions with speed and perform his actions with accuracy.
- If time allows, progress to allowing the secondary striker to follow up looking for rebounds and work on the keeper's reactions to get upright quickly to deal with secondary chances and rebounds.
- Look for the keeper's decision-making, be positive in your advice to him and remind him that goals WILL get scored.

goalkeeper

Functional practice

05. Distribution and playing out from the back (20–25 mins)

Set-up

Set up as a functional practice session. The practice involves the goalkeeper and four teammates, three defenders and a holding or central midfielder, along with three attacking players.

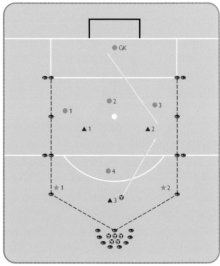

Drill flow

Red 3 plays the ball out of his feet and then plays in to either Red 1 or Red 2 who attempt to shoot at goal. Once the Blue players regain possession, they play to either target (which can be a player, goals or cones). However, the outfield players can only play to the target once it has gone through the keeper. If the keeper makes a save, he can either go direct to a target or play through his teammates.

Key factors

- Ensure the keeper is alert and in the ready position with his nose over his toes and that he is correctly positioned in relation to the goal line, goal and ball (angles).
- Ensure the attackers are direct and positive towards attacking goal.
- Ensure the keeper is alert and ready for shots at all times – does he regularly check his posts to gauge his position?
- Work on the keeper's communication with his teammates, does he tell them where to set their defensive line, to adjust their defensive shape and to close down players to stop shots?
- If the defending team wins the ball, does the keeper communicate to receive the ball in order to relieve the pressure?
- If the keeper does receive a back pass, work on his decision-making on what to do with the ball, if under pressure can he play the ball away to safety upfield?
- If the keeper has the ball in his position from either a save or a back pass, do Blue 1 and 3 go wide to offer outlets to maintain possession. Can Blue 2 and 4 create space to receive the ball?
- Encourage Blue players to maintain possession and not be forced to simply play long and predictably. Can they play with quality out to the targets?
- If time allows, remove the condition on having to play through the keeper and see how this affects the outfield players. Do they simply go long quickly, or can they still play with control to the targets?

Functional practice

06. Dealing with crosses 1 (20–25 mins)
Set-up

Set up as a functional session. The drill involves working on the goalkeeper. Opposition comprises three players who can send in quality crosses, plus two targets (i.e. players, portable goals or cones). If time allows, progress to session two to include two defending centre backs and two attacking strikers (session plan 07).

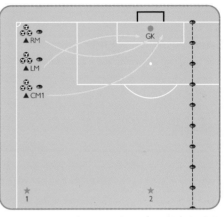

Drill flow

Crosses are played in by the three wide players. The goalkeeper must either collect the cross or call for it to be cleared depending on where the ball arrives in the six-yard box. If the keeper collects the ball, can he play it out with control and accuracy to the two targets?

Key factors

■ Ensure the crosses are of a high quality and primarily delivered into the six-yard box.

■ Ensure that the crossing players mix up their sequence so that the goalkeeper has to keep concentrating.

■ The keeper should work on his body shape and positioning prior to the cross being made. He should have a body shape/angle that allows him to see the ball, his defenders and the attackers. Rather than stand facing the ball, can he stand at 45 degrees so that, with minimal head movement, he can see the whole six-yard box?

■ He should ensure his bodyweight is on the balls of his feet, not his heels, and that he is relaxed and ready to deal with the cross.

■ If the keeper decides to attack the ball, he must leave it late and meet the ball at its highest point.

■ If the keeper collects the ball, can he do it moving forwards so that his bodyweight cushions any impact with defenders or attackers, taking him past the point of contact? Can he go to ground in a controlled manner, keeping the ball under control?

■ If he needs to punch, can he punch through the middle of the ball using strong arms and shoulders and achieve distance over the nearest attacking players to safety?

■ If he needs to deflect the ball, can this be done with distance and width to send the ball to safety?

■ The keeper should assess the flight of the ball, decide his actions early and communicate loudly to his teammates, i.e. 'KEEPER'S' to collect or 'AWAY' if he wants the defenders to deal with the cross.

■ Ensure the keeper tracks the ball at all times, adjusting his position relative to the ball. Once he has collected the ball, can he distribute it with control to the targets?

goalkeeper

Functional practice

07. Dealing with crosses 2 (20–25 mins)
Set-up
Set up as a functional session. The drill involves working on the goalkeeper and the two central defenders. Opposition comprises three players who can send in quality crosses and two strikers to attack goal, plus two targets (i.e. players, portable goals or cones).

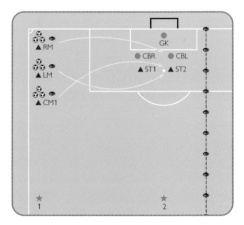

Drill flow
Crosses are played in by any of the three wide players and the goalkeeper must work on either collecting the cross or calling for it to be cleared depending on where the ball arrives in the six-yard box. If the keeper collects the ball, can he play it out with control and accuracy to the two targets?

Key factors
- Ensure the crosses are of a high quality and primarily delivered into the six-yard box.
- Ensure that the crossing players mix up their sequence so that the goalkeeper has to keep concentrating.
- It is important that the keeper works on his body shape and positioning prior to the cross being made. He should look to have a body shape/angle that allows him to see the ball, his defenders and the attackers. Rather than stand facing the ball, can he stand at 45° so that, with minimal head movement, he can see the whole six-yard box?
- He should ensure his bodyweight is on the balls of his feet, not his heels, and that he is relaxed and ready to deal with the cross.
- If the keeper decides to attack the ball, he must leave it late and meet the ball at its highest point.
- If the keeper collects the ball, can he do it moving forwards so that his bodyweight cushions any impact with defenders or attackers, taking him past the point of contact? Can he go to ground in a controlled manner, keeping the ball under control?
- If he needs to punch, can he punch through the middle of the ball using strong arms and shoulders and achieve distance over the nearest attacking players?
- If he needs to deflect the ball, can this be done with distance and width to send the ball into safer areas?
- The keeper should assess the flight of the ball, decide his actions early and communicate loudly to his teammates, i.e. 'KEEPER'S' to collect or 'AWAY' if he wants the defenders to deal with the cross.
- Ensure the keeper tracks the ball at all times, adjusting his position relative to the ball. Once he has collected the ball, can he distribute it with control to the targets?

Small-sided game

08. Shot stopping (20–25 mins)
Set-up
Set up as a small-sided game. The practice involves the goalkeeper and three teammates, against an opposing team of a goalkeeper and three outfield players.

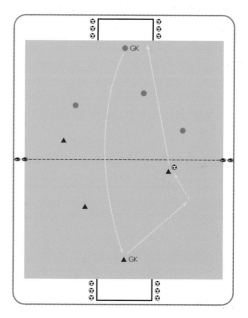

Drill flow
Blue GK throws the ball overarm to Red GK who plays the ball to a teammate. Once the ball is in play, it is free-play with both teams trying to shoot at goal. If a goal is scored, the keeper plays the ball to the opposite keeper and play resumes. As per SSG rules, there are no corners but throw-ins are as normal.

Key factors
- Ensure both teams attack positively, but they defend realistically, i.e. do not all attack at once.
- Ensure the keeper is alert and in the ready position with his nose over his toes and that he is correctly positioned in relation to the goal line and the ball (angles).
- Ensure the keeper is ready for shots – does he regularly check his posts to gauge his position? Does he assume the set position before shots?
- The keeper can block with any part of the body. It is crucial that he remains big for as long as possible to force the attackers to make shooting decisions themselves, i.e. going to ground too early opens up part of the goal.
- If the keeper saves the ball but doesn't hold it, he must send the ball to a safe area either side of the goal and preferably not back into play. If he doesn't hold it, he must react quickly to secondary actions. Can he gather the loose ball or make further saves or blocks?
- Work on the keeper's diving and saving techniques, ensure he doesn't cross his feet to move into line with the ball and he uses his nearest leg to push off. Ensure he has locked wrists and a strong hand for deflections.
- Can the keeper go down the striker's line to narrow the angle? Ensure he gets into the set position before the shot.
- Ensure the keeper communicates to players clearly, concisely and loudly.
- Base these instructions on closing down the ball to prevent strikes at goal. Does the keeper want the defender to show him inside or outside to take him towards other defenders? Does he want his players to drop off and become compact once the opposition have the ball? Where does he want his defenders to be for defensive balance?
- Defenders should keep their shape and balance, especially after a shot at goal.

goalkeeper

Small-sided game

09. Dealing with crosses (20–25 mins)

Set-up

Set up as a small-sided game. The practice involves the goalkeeper and six teammates, against an opposing team of the same make-up. Two channels are marked 6–9m in from the side lines for the four wide players to work in. The area is full pitch width by 36m deep.

Drill flow

Blue GK throws the ball overarm to Red GK who then plays the ball to one of his teammates. Once the ball is in play, it is free play but only the four wide players can be in their channels and they cannot tackle each other. The players outside of the channels must make four passes before they can play it wide, however, if the keeper catches the ball he can throw it directly to a wide player.

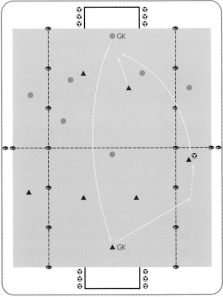

Key factors

- Ensure both teams attack positively, but they defend realistically, i.e. do not all attack at once.
- Ensure the keeper is alert and in the ready position with his nose over his toes and that he is correctly positioned in relation to the goal line and the ball (angles).
- Ensure the keeper is communicating clearly and concisely to the defenders, however, once the ball is crossed in, he must concentrate on the ball alone.
- The keeper should assess the flight of the ball, decide his actions early and then communicate loudly to his teammates, i.e. 'KEEPER'S' to collect or 'AWAY' if he wants the defenders to deal with the cross.
- If the keeper decides to attack the ball, he must leave it late and meet the ball at its highest point.
- If the keeper collects the ball, can he do it moving forwards so that his bodyweight cushions any impact with defenders or attackers, taking him past the point of contact? Can he go to ground in a controlled manner, keeping the ball under control?
- If the keeper does come to collect the ball, the defenders must adopt good defensive positions to block runners and protect the keeper.
- The defenders must hold good positions and try not to be isolated if attackers move across them. They must adopt an open stance to see the ball and the attackers.
- If the ball needs to be cleared, can it be cleared in the direction it came from, so that defenders are still facing the danger, or long and away from danger?
- Keepers must track the ball across the goal. Both the defenders and keeper should deal with secondary chances by adjusting their position quickly to be in line with the ball.

Phase of play

10. Dealing with the back pass and distribution (20–25 mins)
Set-up

Set up as a phase of play. The drill works on the defensive back four, two central midfielders and one striker. Opposition comprises two strikers, the midfield four and the left- and right-back, plus two servers and two targets (i.e. players, portable goals or cones). Progress to include defensive wide midfielders.

Drill flow

Ball is played from Server 1 to Server 2 and then out wide to Red RB or LB, or to Red RM or LM. They play an early ball behind the defence and observe how players react. If the ball goes out of play, normal rules apply, but corners are not awarded.

Key factors

■ Ensure the attacking team play directly, looking to get the ball behind the defenders quickly.

■ Ensure the defending team maintains a high line to create space beyond them.

■ The keeper should remain calm and communicate clearly when dealing with a back pass.

■ He should either communicate to an individual with clear, concise information, or to the team with strong and authoritative information. He must not let this cloud his concentration on the ball.

■ If the keeper calls for a back pass, can he direct the player to pass to a safe position? Can he offer an angle for the pass that does not put him in line with goal?

■ If the keeper receives a back pass, he must assess the quality and direction of the pass. Can he receive it with either foot? Does he have time to control his touch and what kick will he use?

■ Upon the back pass, ensure the defenders move to positions to offer support for short simple passes. If the kick goes long, can they tuck in to offer cover in front of the keeper?

■ If the ball is played over the top, the keeper should judge whether he can collect the ball or if not, he must hold his position.

■ If he decides to go, it must be early, or the attacker could get in. If he does go, can he collect? If he is pressured, can he clear to safety (i.e. the proverbial 'Row Z')?

■ If he decides to stay, he must clearly communicate this to the defenders.

■ If he collects, the defenders and midfield players should assume positions to receive, i.e. fullbacks go wide and higher; central defenders create space to receive the ball; central midfielders drop and offer. Avoid kicking the ball long, and instead work to retain possession.

■ Once the keeper has passed, can he communicate the options that are on, i.e. if played wide, is there a pass to a central player, or up the line to a forward wide player?

defender

Skills practice

11. Basics of 1 v 1 defending (15–20 mins)
Set-up
Set up as a skills practice session. The practice involves the goalkeeper and a defender, along with an attacking player and three servers.

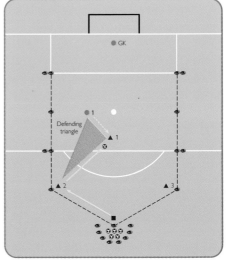

Drill flow
The Server plays the ball to Red 2 or 3 who take a touch and play it to the feet of Red 1. If Red 1 needs to play it back to Red 2 or 3 he can, but they must play it across to each other before playing it back to Red 1. If Blue 1 or the keeper wins the ball, they can play it to Red 2 or 3 and the sessions resets.

Key factors
- Ensure passing between the Servers is crisp and solid and the ball into Red 1 is to his feet.
- Red 1 should be positive and look to attack goal where possible.
- Ensure the keeper is communicating with Blue 1 and is clear and concise.
- Blue 1 must adopt a good stance with his body open to see both the ball and player. He should be half-turned towards the attacker in the correct marking position (if you were to lay it out on the ground, the shape would make a triangle).
- As the ball is travelling between the Server and Red 1, Blue 1 should move towards the attacker so that when the ball is controlled he could lean forwards and touch the player.
- If the pass is under-hit, Blue 1 must decide whether he can intercept the ball. If he can, he must be positive and act immediately. If he can't, he should be patient and adopt the correct marking position.
- If Blue 1 gets too tight to the attacker, a clever attacker will use the defender's body to spin around him. If he is too far away, the attacker will be able to control the ball and open up to attack him. Therefore, once Red 1 has controlled the ball, Blue 1 must maintain a balanced position, with the correct foot forward, using an angled stance so he could touch the player with a straight arm.
- Blue 1 should be patient, force the attacker to make decisions and wait for an opportunity to win the ball.
- The keeper must maintain communication and encourage the defender to be patient. If the defender can't win the ball in a game, all they need to do is delay the attacker until help arrives.
- Once Blue 1 is comfortable with the concept, swap players around so they all get a go.

Skills practice

12. 1 v 1 Defending – forcing play in one direction (15–20 mins)

Set-up

Set up as a skills practice. The practice involves the goalkeeper and a defender, along with an attacking player and three servers.

Drill flow

The Server plays the ball to Red 2 or 3, who takes a touch and plays it to the feet of Blue 1. If Blue 1 needs to play it back to Red 2 or Red 3 he can, but they must play it across to each other before playing it back to Red 1. If Blue 1 or the keeper wins the ball, they play it to Red 2 or 3 and the sessions resets.

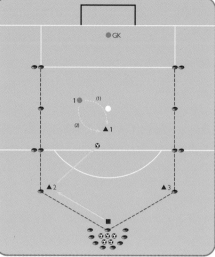

Key factors

- Ensure the passing between the servers is crisp and solid and the ball is to Red 1's feet. Red 1 should be positive and look to attack goal where possible.
- Ensure the keeper is communicating well with Blue 1 and is clear and concise.
- Blue 1 must adopt a good stance with their body open to see both the ball and the player (defending triangle – see p.68).
- As the ball is travelling between Server and Red 2, Blue 1 should move towards the attacker so that when the ball is controlled he could lean forwards and touch the player.
- When making this run, the defender has to decide which way he wants to show the attacker and work in conjunction with the keeper. If the attacker prefers his right foot, then the defender needs to make a curved run to his left (see (1)) to show the attacker on to his left foot. If the attacker prefers his left foot, the defender needs to make a curved run to his right (see (2)) to show the attacker on to his right foot.
- Now working with the keeper the defender must narrow the angle for the shot while still applying pressure. This requires clear and concise communication from the keeper as to where they want the defender to move the attacker.
- If at any time the defender can win or clear the ball, they should be positive and do so.
- Once Blue 1 is comfortable with the concept, swap the players around so they all get a go.

defender

Skills practice

13. 1 v 1 Defending – stop the ball being played forwards or front screening (15–20 mins)

Set-up

Set up as a skills practice. The practice involves the goalkeeper and a defender, along with an attacking player and three servers.

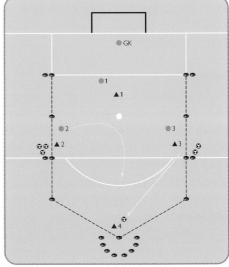

Drill flow

Either Red 2 or 3 plays a pass to Red 4, who looks to link with Red 1. The Blue player defending the opposite Red player, who makes the pass, then looks to close on Red 4.

Key factors

- Ensure the passing between the Red players is crisp and solid and the ball into Red 4 is to their feet.
- All players should be on their toes and looking to play with a high tempo and enthusiasm.
- In the above example, once the ball has been played by Red 3, Blue 2 becomes active and must work to quickly move into the line of vision between Red 4 and 1. To do this, his run must first be across the pitch and into line and then curved.
- The object of this exercise is to provide a 'front screen' in front of the attacker and not to pressure Red 4. By providing this front screen the defender is looking to restrict the options of the player on the ball and generate time for the team, or to make the attacking team play in a predictable direction.
- If Red 4 does hesitate, then Blue 2 can edge forwards to apply more pressure and unsettle Red 4. Communication is now essential between Blue 1 and 2 to ensure Blue 2 remains in the line of sight between the two attackers.
- If Blue 2 can win the ball, he should be positive and either win the ball or put it out of play.
- If the ball is played into the feet of Red 1, Red 4 becomes passive and Blue 2 can spin to help Blue 1 defend Red 1.
- Once the defenders are comfortable with the concept, swap the players around so all players attempt front screening.
- If time allows, let Red 4 play forwards and work on the defensive positioning and body shape of the screening play to maintain balance and the correct stance.

Skills practice

14. 1 v 2 Defending – delaying play when outnumbered (15–20 mins)

Set-up
Set up as a skills practice. The practice involves the goalkeeper and a defender, along with two attacking players and a server.

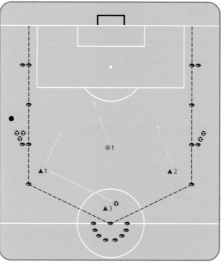

Drill flow
Red 3 takes a touch out of his feet and then passes to either Red 1 or 2. Both Red 1 and 2 attack the goal and Blue 1 has to drop and defend. If Blue 1 or the keeper wins possession they should clear to Red 3.

Key factors
- This drill is demanding, so ensure that Blue and Red players rotate or are given a rest so that the drill is always carried out at a high tempo.
- Ensure the keeper is communicating well with Blue 1 and is clear and concise. The keeper needs to decide how deep he wants Blue 1 to drop, i.e. 10m outside the area, edge of the area etc.
- Blue 1 must hold a central position. As the ball is played from Red 3 to one of the two attacking players, Blue 1 needs to start to drop to allow himself the time to recover backwards, with an open stance so that he can see both players. Blue 1 should try and avoid having to turn his back to make his recovery run, as he will lose sight of at least one of the attackers.
- Blue 1 must give ground at a rate that means the attackers have to make decisions. If he retreats too quickly he will give them open space to run in to. If he retreats too slowly, he will allow them to pass past him and the other striker to get goal-side.
- If the keeper feels a shot is going to be made, he must communicate for Blue 1 to apply enough pressure to force the shot, but not so much that he commits himself and allows a clever striker to check his shot and pass to the second attacker who would then be clear.
- Therefore, Blue 1's approach needs to be angled to stop the square pass, but also to narrow the angle of the shot and help the keeper.
- Also, Blue 1 should try and make the far post shot difficult by blocking off this part of the goal and therefore allowing the keeper to cover only his near post.
- Above all, Blue 1 must be patient. By making the attackers slow down their attack, Blue 1 is allowing other defenders time to recover and help.

defender

Skills practice

15. 2 v 2 – recovering runs from the wrong side of the ball (15–20 mins)

Set-up

Set up as a skills practice. The practice involves the goalkeeper and two defenders, along with two attacking players and a server.

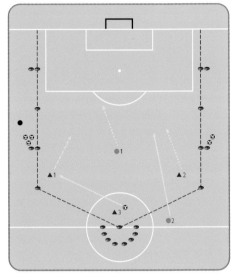

Drill flow

Red 3 takes a touch off their feet and then passes to Red 1 or 2. Once this pass is made, Blue 2 can drop to help defend. Both Red 1 and 2 attack the goal and Blue 1 and 2 have to combine to defend. If the Blue players win possession, can they clear to Red 3?

Key factors

- This drill is demanding, so ensure that Blue and Red players rotate or rest so that the drill is always carried out at a high tempo.
- Ensure the keeper is communicating well with the defenders – Blue 1 in particular – and is clear and concise. The keeper needs to decide how deep he wants Blue 1 to drop, i.e. 10m outside the area, edge of the area etc.
- Blue 1 must hold a central position. As the ball is played from Red 3 to one of the two attacking players, Blue 1 should start dropping to allow himself the time to recover, with an open stance to see both players. Blue 1 should avoid having to turn his back to make his recovery run, as he will lose sight of at least one of the attackers.
- Blue 1 must give ground at a rate that forces the attackers to make decisions. If he retreats too quickly he gives them open space to run into, if he retreats too slowly, he allows them to pass him and the other striker to get goal-side.
- If Blue 2 is furthest from the ball (see above), then his run needs to be to the back of the defence so he becomes the supporting defender and allows Blue 1 to apply pressure. If Blue 2 is nearest to the ball, he must work hard to become the primary defender applying pressure. Once Blue 1 has slowed the attackers he becomes the support defender.
- If the keeper feels a shot will be made, he must communicate to the closest defender to apply pressure and narrow the angle. This approach should be angled to stop the square pass, but also to narrow the angle of the shot. The defender should try and make the far post shot difficult by blocking this part of the goal, leaving the keeper to cover the near post only.

Technical practice

16. Defensive heading (15–20 mins)
Set-up
Set up as a technical practice. The drill involves working with two teams of two players and the practice area is two equal squares.

Drill flow
Blue 2 serves the ball up to Blue 1 who uses a high defensive header to create as much height, direction and distance as possible. The Red players can return the ball, but it must be with a header.

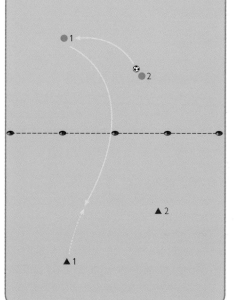

Key factors
- Ensure the players are heading up through the ball in a defensive manner and not down on to the ball, as in an attacking header.
- Ensure the player heading the ball has his eyes open, looking at the ball.
- His body stance should be balanced on both feet with his bodyweight on the balls of his feet.
- Can he meet and power through the bottom half of the ball and upwards to generate power and distance on the header?
- To help the players generate power, have them imagine that they have their arms on a bar in front of them, at the point of heading the ball. Can they pull forwards on this bar and use their back, shoulder and neck muscles to generate full power?
- Encourage the players to name the ball as their own, but ensure they keep their mouths closed as they head the ball so as not to bite their tongues.
- Work on their body stance and positioning so that they can head through the ball and get the direction they are aiming for, either front on or slightly angled, and twist their heads to set the direction.
- As the ball is travelling towards them, they must adjust their body positioning early to get themselves set, and then use small balancing steps to get to the ball to be in the correct position and stance.
- Encourage the players to attack the ball and not simply to let it hit their head. Ensure they always make good positive movements towards the ball to give themselves the confidence to make a good strong header.

defender

Skills practice

17. Defensive heading – head tennis (15–20 mins)
Set-up
Set up as a skills practice. The drill involves working with two teams of four players – three defending, one attacking – and the practice area is two equal squares.

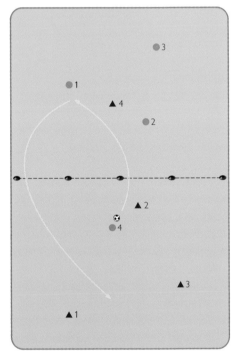

Drill flow
Blue 4 serves the ball to Blue 1, 2 or 3, who use a high defensive header to create as much height, direction and distance as possible. The Red players try to return the ball with a header that clears the back of the opposition team's grid. Each team has alternate service. The attackers are passive at first.

Key factors
- Ensure the players are heading up through the ball in a defensive manner and not down on to the ball, as in an attacking header.
- Ensure the players are in an alert and ready stance and have the weight on the balls of their feet so they can react quickly to the direction of the incoming ball.
- Each player needs to judge the line and flight of the ball and the nearest player needs to communicate their intentions early. If they can meet the ball, they need to call their name early and not use a call of 'mine', which may result in a free kick in a game. If they cannot get to the ball, they need to move out of the way and communicate this.
- If a player does call for the ball, the other players need to ensure they remain alert to whether the danger is dealt with, as they may need to clear the ball with a secondary header.
- Encourage the players to attack the ball and not simply to let it hit their head. Ensure they always make good positive movements towards the ball to give themselves the confidence to make a strong header.
- Once the danger has been dealt with, the players need to be switched on and ready for the next attack. They need communicate with each other to ensure they have a good defensive structure and are not, for instance, all at the back or front of the grid.
- Once they have this structure, they then need to concentrate on their own body shape so that they can see the ball and the attacker – defensive triangle (see p.68).

Small-sided game

18. Defensive heading (20–25 mins)
Set-up
Set up as a small-sided game session. The drill involves working with one team on their defensive heading technique and defensive shape. Teams should ideally contain seven or eight players and both the pitch and the goals should suit the age of the players.

Drill flow
Teams start in the structured start position. The team being coached starts with the ball and players throw, head and catch the ball in that sequence. In the example, Blue 4 throws the ball to Blue 6 who heads it for Blue 5 to catch. If the ball touches the ground it is lost and opposing players cannot catch the ball, but if they head it they win possession, even if the other team catches the ball.

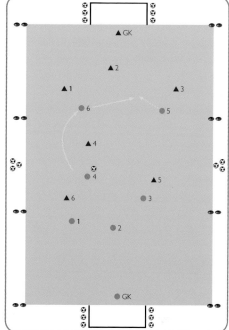

Key factors
- Ensure that play is at a high tempo and that defensively the teams keep a realistic structure and shape.
- As a coach, you are looking to observe what happens when the ball is lost and how the players react.
- The first line of communication must come from the keeper who can see everything that is happening. The keeper must ensure that the players nearest to him keep their shape and structure.
- When the ball is lost, all the players must react and take up a defensive shape on the player nearest to them. This shape should allow them to see the ball and the attacker i.e. defensive triangle (see p.68).
- When the ball is thrown into their area, the player must ensure that they immediately pressurise the attacker and go to meet the ball first.
- The keeper must communicate clearly and concisely. If they can claim the ball, they must do so and communicate this by shouting 'KEEPER'S'. If they cannot, they must shout 'AWAY' or 'CLEAR'.
- Players must react to the keeper's communication. If the keeper calls for the ball, can they block runners to give the keeper some protection? If the keeper shouts clear, can they deal with the danger?
- Players and the keeper need to keep the communication going at all times. If the ball is won and the play moves up the field, can the keeper and the back two defenders work to keep the team's shape and structure?

defender

Functional practice

19. Defensive shape when outnumbered (20–25 mins)
Set-up

Set up as a functional practice. This involves working with one team on their defensive shape when they are outnumbered. Include the keeper and four defenders along with five attackers, two servers and two targets (e.g. players, goals or cones). Use the full width of the pitch, down to the halfway line (the goals should suit the age of the players).

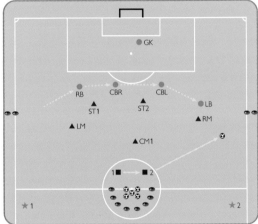

Drill flow

The ball is played from Server 1 to 2 and then either out wide to Red RM or Red LM, or through the middle to Red CM. Let the play run for several phases to observe how the players react. If the ball goes out of play, normal rules apply, but corners are not awarded.

Key factors

- Ensure the drill is carried out at a fast tempo, and that attacking players are positive and direct.
- The first line of communication must come from the keeper, who can see all of the action. He must ensure that the players keep their shape and structure.
- See above. The ball has been played wide to attacking Red RM. The defending Blue LB has decided to apply pressure, so both centre backs have moved across to supply cover and balance. The defending Blue RB has tucked in to maintain shape.
- If the ball was switched across field, all defenders could pendulum to the opposite side while the ball was travelling, yet maintain their structure.
- The keeper can communicate this and tell the defenders where to hold their line, or when to drop off or retreat, pressure or move across and tuck in.
- The defensive unit should communicate clearly so that they push out, drop and move across together.
- The player nearest the ball needs to decide early whether to press or hold and when to cover space. If the ball is played into a striker who drops deep, and the centre back applies pressure, the other centre back and two full backs needs to tuck in to stop gaps appearing. If the ball is then moved on, they can realign and decide how to pressure the ball.
- If a player is out of position, he needs to assess to where his recovery run should go. If a player has covered his position can he fall back into another good defensive position to allow the unit to reshape once the pressure is cleared?
- All defenders should work on their body shape e.g. defending triangle (see p.68), to see the ball and attackers. They must not ball watch and allow players to make runs in behind them.
- If they win the ball, coach them to play out with control and composure to the targets.

Functional practice

20. Defensive shape and compactness (20–25 mins)
Set-up
Set up as a functional practice. The drill involves working with one team on their defensive central midfield shape. Includes the keeper, two centre backs, a central midfielder and two wide midfielders along with five attackers, two servers and two targets (e.g. players, goals or cones). Use the width of the penalty area to just in front of the halfway line. Goals should suit the age of the players.

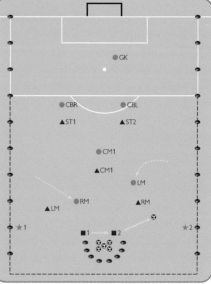

Drill flow
The ball is played from Server 1 to 2 and then out to either Red RM or LM, or through the middle to Red CM. Let the play run for a couple of phases to observe how the players react. If the ball goes out of play, normal rules apply, but corners are not awarded.

Key factors
- Ensure the drill is carried out at a fast tempo, and that attacking players are positive and direct.
- The first line of communication must come from the keeper, who can see all of the action. He should ensure that he has a good position in relation to play and encourages the defenders to push up and hold a high line.
- The communication of the defensive unit must be clear and concise so that all players can react quickly. The players must be confident to hold their defensive positions and not force play.
- See above. The ball has been played wide to the attacking Red RM. The defending Blue LM has decided to both apply pressure and front screen (see p.70) Red ST2. The defending Blue RM has also tucked in to screen the attacking Red LM and now Red RM has limited options open to him.
- If the attacking team recycle the ball and play away, the keeper must be proactive and ask his defenders to push up as well.
- All defenders should work on their body shape e.g. defending triangle (see p.68), to see the ball and attackers. They must not ball watch and allow players to make runs behind them.
- If play is switched to the left, the three midfielders must work as a unit to 'front screen' the dangerous attacking players (Red ST1 and 2) and, where possible, the central midfield player. All players should be switched on to work this defending principle.
- By achieving this compactness, the defending unit can make play predictable and simply move across the pitch as the opposition look to switch play or deal with any balls played long over the top.
- The two centre backs and the holding midfielder must avoid pushing up alone and creating a 'saw tooth'.

defender

Functional practice

21. Tracking runners (20–25 mins)
Set-up
Set up as a functional practice. The drill involves working with one team on their defensive central midfield shape. Include a keeper, two centre backs and two central midfielders along with four attackers and two wide attackers who work only in their zones, plus two servers and two targets (e.g. players, goals or cones). Use the width of the penalty area plus two outside zones, to just in front of the halfway line.

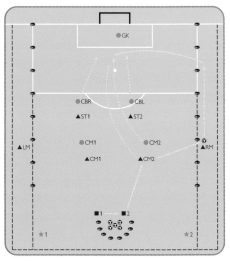

Drill flow
The ball is played from Server 1 to 2 and then out to either midfielder who in turn plays it wide to either of the two wide midfielders. The wide midfielder travels up the line and crosses in from different positions.

Key factors
- Ensure the drill is carried out at a fast tempo, and that attacking players are positive and direct.
- Each defender must work on their body stance and positioning i.e. defending triangle (see p.68) so that they can see the ball, wide player and the player they are marking.
- When a midfield defender is tracking a runner, he must follow the player all the way to the back of the defence, but must be aware not to go past the last defender as he will play everyone else onside.
- See above. The ball has been played into Red CM2 who has in turn played it wide to Red RM. He has made a run upfield and crossed the ball into the penalty area. Once Red CM2 has made his pass, they have made a strong run into the area and Blue CM2 has tracked them back all the way, getting in front of the player to deal with the cross.
- The defenders must also make good decisions on whether to mark the players closely or to cover space to allow other defenders to attack the ball.
- The keeper needs to keep up a good line of communication, especially with the two centre backs, to help clear the danger at crosses, but he must also know when to concentrate on the cross.
- The players must be aware that at times they will lose sight of the ball, especially when they are sprinting to track an opposition run. As soon as the can, they need to make contact with the ball and, where possible, take up a good defending triangle.

Functional practice

22. Defensive cover and balance (20–25 mins)
Set-up
Set up as a functional practice. The drill involves working with one team on their defensive shape. Include the keeper, the back four and a central midfielder, along with five attackers, two servers and two targets (e.g. players, goals or cones). Use the width of the penalty area to just in front of the halfway line. Goals should suit the age of the players.

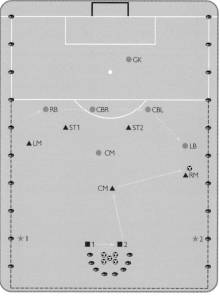

Drill flow
The ball is played from Server 1 to 2 and then out to Red CM, who plays it to Red RM or LM. Let the play run for several phases to observe players' reactions. If the ball goes out of play, normal rules apply, but corners are not awarded.

Key factors
- Ensure the drill is carried out at a fast tempo, and that attacking players are positive and direct.
- Work on units of two or three players to establish the patterns and structure you want to achieve, and then widen it to all five defending players.
- The first line of communication must come from the keeper, who can see all of the action.
- If the ball is high up the pitch and the defenders have pushed high, can the keeper hold a position at the front of the penalty area?
- Defenders should work on their body shape e.g. defending triangle (see p.66). They must not ball watch, allowing players to run behind them.
- As soon as the ball is played, the defenders must pre-empt the next pass, then decide on their actions. Does the nearest defender apply pressure or not? If he does, will the second nearest defender move into a supporting position? How do the other defenders react?
- See above. The ball is played to Red CM who then plays to Red RM. The defending Blue LB decides to apply pressure, so the Blue CBL moves across to provide support.
- Blue CBR now has responsibilities: providing support to the left back, being aware of the nearest striker and assessing the nearby danger, reacting accordingly.
- The furthest defender should maintain position. See above. Blue RB has 'tucked across' to provide support marking Red ST1. If the ball is played across field to Red LM, he can move across – as will all the players – and realign his position.
- The players' unit should work out a range of calls to communicate their actions with minimal words, i.e. 'tuck in', 'hold the line', 'pressure', 'show inside' or 'show outside' etc.
- Depending on their shape, defenders can show attackers inside or out to send them into this support.

defender

Phase of play

23. Roles and responsibilities in the defending third (20–25 mins)

Set-up

Set up as a phase of play. The drill involves working on the defensive back four, two central midfielders and one of the strikers. Opposition comprises two strikers, the midfield four and two fullbacks, plus two servers and two targets (e.g. players, portable goals or cones). If numbers allow, progress to include defensive wide midfielders.

Drill flow

The ball is played from Server 1 to 2 and then out wide to Red RM or LM, or through the middle to Red CM1 or CM2. Let the play run for several phases to observe how the players react. If the ball goes out of play, normal rules apply, but corners are not awarded.

Key factors

- Ensure the drill is carried out at a fast tempo and attacking players are positive and realistic.
- The whole shape of the defence is decided by the actions of the nearest player. If they decide to press the attacker with the ball, the rest of the defence must react accordingly. Communication is essential and must start from the goalkeeper, progressing through the team.
- See above. The ball has been played to the attacking right midfielder. The defending left back decided to press the player in possession, so the centre backs and, most importantly, the right back have to move across and ensure a good defensive shape.
- The two defending central midfielders must drop and screen the two attacking strikers. Blue CM2 should drop in front of Red ST2, but also look to cover the attacking right midfielder. Blue CM1 should drop in front of the two strikers to attempt to intercept any passes to the two strikers.
- The defending striker should drop to provide cover and balance in the midfield and therefore become the player that can apply pressure to the two attacking central midfielders should the ball be played to them.
- If either of the central midfielders make attacking runs into the attacking third, then the defending central midfielder must look to track this run all the way to ensure the attackers do not become undefended in the danger areas.
- The fullback furthest from play must deal with any balls played to the back post. His body position must be open, keeping both the ball and the opposition in view.
- If the nearest defender presses when the ball is played into the feet of either striker, the remaining three must close up, maintaining defensive balance.
- If the ball is won, can it be played out with control to the targets?

Phase of play

24. Roles and responsibilities in the attacking third (20–25 mins)

Set-up

Set up as a phase of play. The drill involves working on the defensive duties of the strikers, midfielders and two fullbacks. Opposition comprises the keeper and back four, plus the two central midfielders and one of their strikers, two servers and two targets (e.g. players, portable goals or cones).

Drill flow

The ball is played from Server 1 to 2 and then out wide to Blue RB or LB, who then plays a diagonal ball in behind the defence. Let the play run for several phases to observe players' reactions. If the ball goes out of play, normal rules apply, but corners are not awarded.

Key factors

- Ensure the drill is carried out at a fast tempo. The defending team should play out, rather than thumping the ball long.
- The Blues make the decision on whether to apply pressure or not as soon as the ball is lost.
- If pressure can be applied, the nearest defender must close down the opposition player, preventing them from playing the ball forwards or turning. The opponent should have to concentrate on the ball and shouldn't have time to look up to find options.
- Communication from players with a good field of vision is essential (a centre back or the goalkeeper, if they are high enough).
- Supporting players must combine to apply pressure and limit the options available to the player on the ball.
- Players not involved must shift across to compact play and assume a good potential attacking position.
- Players can be bold when applying pressure in the attacking third. However, if the opposition regain their composure and structure, defenders must not force them and risk losing shape, but rather accept the opportunity is gone, dropping to regain position.
- See above. The ball has been played behind the defence and the opposing goalkeeper has collected and played it out to Red RB. Blue LM has made a curved run to stop Red RB playing the ball up the wing. Blue ST1 has made a run to front screen (see p.70) Red CBR. Blue ST2 has done the same to screen Red CBL and Blue RM has tucked in tight to make the formation compact. Blue CM1 has made a run to front screen Red CM1. Blue CM2 has moved to a good defensive position behind the two opposition midfielders. Blue RB has tucked across to make the whole unit compact.
- Red RB's options are to play through the keeper (high risk with both strikers pushing high) or force a long ball that the centre backs can deal with.
- Early decisions and actions are essential to achieve the pressure!

defender

Small-sided game

25. Defensive shape and reactions when the ball is lost (20–25 mins)
Set-up

Set up as a small-sided game. The drill involves working with the Blue team on their concentration and decisions once they've lost the ball. Teams should ideally contain seven or eight players.

Drill flow

Teams start in the structured start position and the Blue team start with the ball. Let the drill flow for a couple of phases to settle players and once possession has been lost in the opposition half, introduce the coaching points. If the ball goes out of play, normal rules apply, but corners are not awarded.

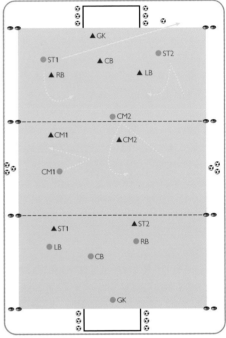

Key factors

- Ensure that teams keep their structure, and play is realistic and played at a high tempo.
- Whenever the ball is lost, concentration can be affected. If the keeper makes a great save, the striker will naturally reflect on their miss, but if the keeper then reacts quickly to get the ball back in play, the striker is not able to affect the game. If a free kick is given and the guilty player argues the point, but the kick is taken quickly, they are now out of the game etc.
- The coach must instil the notion that as soon as the ball is lost, players must assess where and when it will come back into play.
- Players must immediately move into good defensive position i.e. defending triangle (see p.68).
- Players with a good field of vision must convey this information to all players and should communicate the team defensive patterns and structure.
- As soon as the ball is in play, the nearest player should decide if he will apply pressure or not. Based on this decision the remaining players will react by either pressurising or dropping off and becoming compact. Teams that do not have this loss of concentration will keep their shape and deny the opposition the chance to counter-attack quickly.
- See above. Blue ST1 has seen the shot go wide, but immediately drops into a good position behind the opponent. Blue ST2, who was following in for the rebound, loops around to cover Red LB. Blue CM2, who was pushing in to support the front two, drops behind the opposition Red CM2. Blue CM1 had picked up a good position to offer balance, but due to the reaction of his midfield partner, he now tucks in behind Red CM1 and also screens Red ST1, giving the Blue team a great compact shape.

Small-sided game

26. Recovering and retreating when not in possession (20–25 mins)

Set-up

Set up as a small-sided game. The drill involves working with the Blue team on their decision-making and retreating runs once the ball has been lost. Teams should ideally contain seven or eight players.

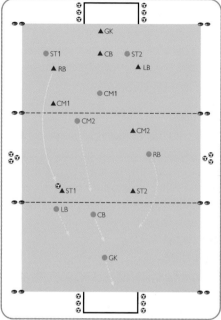

Drill flow

Teams start in the structured start position and the Blue team starts with the ball. Let the drill flow for several phases to settle players. Once possession has been lost in the opposition half, introduce the coaching points. If the ball goes out of play, normal rules apply, but corners are not rewarded.

Key factors

■ Ensure that teams keep their structure, and play is realistic and played at a high tempo.

■ When outnumbered, players have difficult choices to make. Should they apply pressure, hold their position or give ground and retreat?

■ If they hold their ground or apply pressure, but don't win the ball, the opponents could be through on goal. However, if they retreat or give ground, they force the opposition to make decisions, which could lead to poor passes and wrong decision-making, resulting in the ball being cleared or slowing down play and allowing recovery runs to be made.

■ The key element in these decisions is communication. The goalkeeper is best placed to communicate along with supporting players who are trying to recover.

■ Players making the recovery runs should decide if they will pressure the ball or allow the retreating player to pressure, instead taking up a supporting position. It depends on whether they are nearer to the ball than the retreating player.

■ Once the recovering player has assumed position, he must not let his concentration slip, but defend solidly until more help arrives or the ball is cleared to safety.

■ Players must learn that they do not need to get to 'their' position, but simply into a position to assist, i.e. running at angles to the ball to take up a better defensive position.

■ See above. Blue ST1 has lost the ball and it has been played quickly to Red ST1. Blue LB and CB have started to retreat, upon good communication from the keeper. Blue RB, who is the furthest defender, is working hard to get to the back of the defence and offer support. Blue CM2 makes a direct run to cover Red CM2. If the tactics of Blue LB and CB delay Red ST1, the Blue team may be able to regain their shape and avert the danger.

defender

Small-sided game

27. Defending high or dropping to become compact (20–25 mins)

Set-up
Set up as a small-sided game. The drill involves working with the Blue team on their decision-making once the ball has been lost. Do they press to win the ball or drop deep and become compact? Teams should ideally contain seven or eight players.

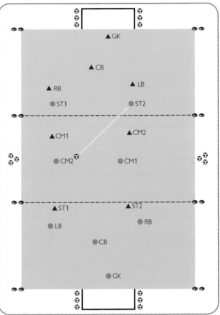

Drill flow
Teams start in the structured start position and the Blue team start with the ball. Let the drill flow for several phases to settle players and, once possession has been lost in the opposition half, introduce the coaching points. If the ball goes out of play, normal rules apply, but corners are not awarded.

Key factors
- Ensure that teams keep their structure, and play is realistic and played at a high tempo.
- In this practice the coach's aim is to generate a team attitude to defending – they must defend as a unit from front to back, with the strikers as the first line of defence.
- Communication from all players with a good field of vision is essential. The whole defensive pattern should come from the nearest defender to the ball.
- The decision on how to defend will depend on where the ball was lost and how many players had gone forward to support the attack. Were a small number of players involved, as it was a quick counter-attack?
- If the ball has been lost high and is played out to an opposition defender, can the strikers or wide midfielders apply pressure to stop them playing forwards? If so, the rest of the team must react positively as a unit to make the defence compact and high to try and win the ball.
- Communication from the keeper through the defenders and on to the midfield is vital. The keeper must adopt a high position to deal with any balls that are played over the top of the defence, acting as a sweeper.
- If this pressure cannot be generated, the midfield must get compact i.e. defending triangle (see p.68) and the two strikers can look to front screen the midfield (see p.70).
- If the individual nearest to the ball cannot apply pressure, they should limit forward passes and look to make the opposition play backwards so all other players can recover their good defensive positions.
- If the decision is to drop, the keeper must tell the defenders how deep to drop, and where to stop and apply pressure.
- Can one of the strikers hold the line of the last defender's shoulder to offer an outlet if the ball is won? If it is played to him, can he hold the ball until support arrives or be positive and attack goal?

Small-sided game

28. Intercepting the ball and breaking up play (20–25 mins)
Set-up
Set up as a small-sided game. The drill involves working with the Blue team on their speed of recovery to a good defensive position and their decision-making on where to intercept the ball. Teams should ideally contain seven or eight players.

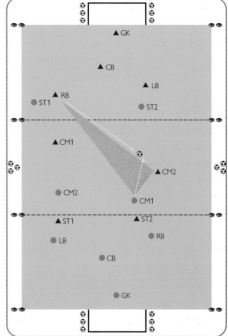

Drill flow
Teams start in the structured start position and the Blue team start with the ball. Let the drill flow for several phases to settle players. Once possession has been lost in the opposition half, introduce the coaching points. If the ball goes out of play, normal rules apply, but corners are not awarded.

Key factors
- Ensure that teams maintain structure, and play is realistic and at a high tempo.
- The aim of this session is to ensure that the Blue players take up a good defensive position quickly so that they can intercept the ball. The whole process starts from their taking up a good defensive position and body stance, i.e. defending triangle (see p.68).
- Once the player has a chance to intercept the ball, work on their decision-making. If they try to intercept and miss, will it leave them badly exposed or are they in a lower risk area where teammates can cover them?
- Players should evaluate the chances of intercepting and where these opportunities will arise: is the pass over a long distance, not hit hard enough, misplaced or in the wrong direction? Does the player making the pass make it obvious where it is going? Has the receiving player showed poor touches to date? Might he have difficulty controlling the ball? Is the risk reward situation high, i.e. are you in the attacking third? Is the cover good and the communication clear so you know you can take the chance?
- The player should also assess if the risk is worth it if they are in their own defending third, if they are the last defender or there is no cover behind, or if they feel they only have a 50/50 chance or less at best.
- See above. Red RB has intercepted the ball, and is looking to pass to Red CM2. Blue CM1 has taken up a good defensive position and has developed a good defending triangle of vision. Communication from both Blue CB and RB informs him that he has good cover.
- The pass is long and slightly under weighted so Blue CM1 takes the opportunity and intercepts. Having won the ball he is three-on-three in attack and the rewards are potentially high.

defender

Small-sided game

29. Marking players and tracking runners (20–25 mins)
Set-up
Set up as a small-sided game. The drill involves working with the Blue team on their shape and structure when different players join the attack. Teams should ideally contain seven or eight players.

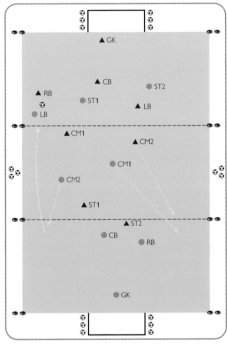

Drill flow
Teams start in the structured start position and the Blue team starts with the ball. Let the drill flow for several phases to settle players. Once possession has been lost in the opposition half, introduce the coaching points. If the ball goes out of play, normal rules apply, but not corners.

Key factors
- Ensure that teams maintain structure, and play is realistic and at a high tempo.
- The coach works to develop the key defenders' understanding of their roles and responsibilities and how other players react when these defenders join the attack to ensure the structure and shape is not lost and the team potentially exposed.
- See above. The attacking Blue LB has made a strong run up the wing to support Blue ST1 and Blue CM2 has shown good vision by dropping wide to cover Blue LB.
- The second phase works on the forward runs of the opposition players. If an opposing midfielder makes a strong run into the danger area, they must be tracked all the way back to ensure the other players can concentrate on marking their players.
- See above. Blue LB has lost the ball to Red RB. Red CM2 has made a strong run wide to look for the through ball. However, Blue CM1 has tracked this player all the way back and put pressure on their pass. If Red RB does make the pass, Blue CM1 is well placed to deal with the threat. Alternatively, Red RB may simply make the short pass to Red CM1 and the Blue team can then react to this threat.
- Ensure that the players do not ball watch, but adopt a good defensive position.
- If the defence does find itself outnumbered, they need to recognise the danger and decide on how to deal with this.

Small-sided game
30. Defensive shape and balance (20–25 mins)
Set-up

Set up as a small-sided game session. The drill involves working with the Blue team to make decisions on how they want to defend once the ball has been lost. Teams should ideally contain seven or eight players.

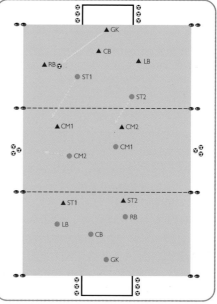

Drill flow

Teams start in the structured start position and the Blue team start with the ball. Let the drill flow for several phases to settle players. Once possession has been lost in the opposition half, introduce the coaching points. If the ball goes out of play, normal rules apply, but corners are not awarded.

Key factors

- Ensure that teams maintain structure, and play is realistic and at a high tempo.
- This drill is an ideal progression from session 24 or any other defensive shape session. The coach's aim is to generate a team attitude to defending. They must defend as a unit from front to back, with the strikers the first line of defence.
- Communication from all players with a good field of vision is essential. The whole defensive pattern comes from the nearest defender to the ball.
- If the ball is lost high and is played out to an opposition defender, can the strikers or wide midfielders apply pressure to stop them playing forwards? If they can, the rest of the team must react to make the defence compact and high to try and win the ball.
- If this pressure cannot be generated, the midfield must get compact, i.e. defending triangle (see p.68) and the two strikers should front screen the midfield (see p.70).
- If the player nearest to the ball cannot apply pressure, they should limit forward passes and look to make the opposition play backwards, so all other players can recover their good defensive positions.
- Both strikers should not drop too deep, because if the ball is won, an outlet is needed to counter-attack quickly. One striker should hold the line of the last defender's shoulder to offer this outlet and he can then drop to create space to receive the ball.
- See above. The ball has been lost and Blue ST1 is too isolated to apply pressure, so instead he drops to screen the midfield. Blue ST2 also screens the other opposition midfielder and Blue CM2 goes slightly wider to prevent balls being played down the line to the opposition striker. Blue CM1 is already in a position to screen Red ST2 and will know this from communication with Blue RB.
- The team should be patient and let the opposition play in their own defensive third, which doesn't cause danger.

attacker

Technical practice

31. Controlling to the safe side (15–20 mins)
Set-up
Set up as a technical practice. The drill involves working with four attacking players against one defender. The size of the area is 12m x 12m.

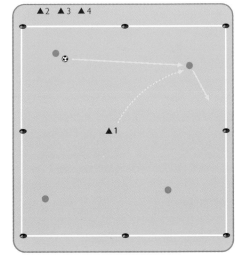

Drill flow
The Blue players pass the ball between them and try to avoid the defender winning the ball. If the defender does win the ball, he plays it to a Red player off the pitch and it is then given back to the Blue players.

Key factors
- Ensure the Red players are rotated regularly to maintain a good tempo, as this exercise can get very tiring.
- The aim of this session is to get the players used to controlling the ball away from approaching defenders, and hence to the 'safe side'.
- Ensure the Blue players are alert, on the balls of their feet and ready to receive the ball, but also relaxed both physically and mentally.
- As the pass is made to them, can the player assess the movement of the defender and then control the ball in a direction away from the approaching defender?
- As the players become more confident in receiving the ball and controlling to the safe side, can they start to introduce disguise, i.e. fake to control one way and then go the other, feint to use one side of the foot, then control with the opposite side etc?
- Once they have controlled the ball and played away, can they play with heads up to decide on the correct pass to make? Is it a simple pass to the player they are moving towards, or can they change the direction of play with a diagonal ball?
- As the players' confidence increases, can they increase the tempo of the drill and look to use two touches to control and pass or one touch when the pass is on?
- Ensure that the players are all communicating with each other, calling out the teammate's name to which they are passing, and communicating where the space is and when to give or keep hold of the ball.
- Once the Blue players are comfortable, swap for the Red players. The Blue players become the defenders.
- If time allows and both sets of players have had a turn, introduce a second defender and watch the decision-making of the receiving player.

Technical practice

32. Pass selection and decision-making (15–20 mins)

Set-up
Set up as a technical practice. The drill involves working with the Blue team of eight players on their decision-making and pass selection. The opposition is four defenders. The size of the area is 18m x 18m.

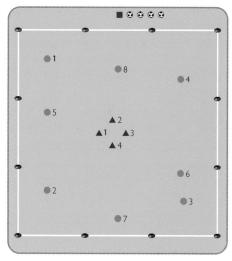

Drill flow
The server plays the ball into a Blue player. Between them they must try and avoid losing the ball to the defenders. Can they make 10 passes without losing the ball? If the defenders win the ball, can they make five passes without losing it?

Key factors
- Ensure the Red players are rotated regularly to maintain a good tempo, as this exercise can get very tiring.
- Ensure that when the Blue players have possession they play with their heads up and observe the positioning and movement of players around them.
- Do players have an open body stance, to see the ball and the players? Are they ready to receive the ball and alert to any opportunity?
- As the pass is made to them, can the player assess the movement of the defender and then control the ball in a direction away from the approaching defender? If they are closed down by two defenders this may mean that the safe side is through the defenders.
- Can they use disguise to mask their intentions and feints to put defenders off balance?
- Work on their decision-making once they have controlled the ball. What type of pass do they use? Can they run into space to commit defenders before passing? Can they use cross-field balls to change the direction of play before they become crowded out?
- When the player does not have the ball, can they create angles and space to receive the pass? Can they feint one way and then change direction to make space and call for the pass?
- Can the player on the ball and their nearest supporting player be creative by making close runs past each other and either taking the ball or leaving the ball to confuse defenders?
- When they lose possession and then regain it, what are the decisions of the Blue players? Do they look to create space? How do they communicate? Can they make several short passes to work the ball out of a danger area and then relax?
- Once the Blue players are comfortable with the drill, swap the defenders around. Alternatively, make three teams – the team who loses the ball, becomes the defenders.

attacker

Skills practice

33. Technique of ball control (15–20 mins)

Set-up

Set up as a skills practice. The drill involves working with one Blue player and a server who can make high quality passes over 25–30m. The opposition is two defenders. The size of the area is 18m x 30m.

Drill flow

The server plays the ball out of their feet and then hits a lofted pass to the Blue player, who uses different parts of his body to control the ball. Initially pressure is applied passively by one of the defenders, but as the practice progresses either both defenders can press or one can try to win the ball.

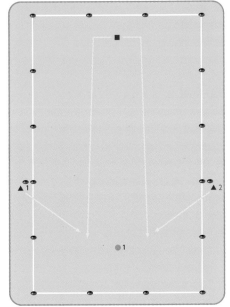

Key factors

- Ensure the passing in is of a high quality otherwise the drill will lose focus.
- Ensure that the receiving player is alert and ready to receive the ball. He should be both mentally and physically relaxed.
- As the ball is played from the server, can Blue 1 move into the line of flight of the ball and take small balancing steps to set himself?
- As the ball is in flight, can Blue 1 judge how high it will reach him and then decide early what controlling surface he will use?
- As the ball arrives, can Blue 1 watch the ball onto the controlling surface and keep his head steady?
- As he controld the ball, can he play the ball to the safe side (see p.88) away from the defender?
- Once Blue 1 has controlled the ball to the safe side, can he play with heads up to see the server and then make a pass down the line to the server with accuracy and pace?
- As Blue 1 becomes more comfortable with the drill, can he start to introduce some disguise to his control to put the defender off balance and some feints to make time for the pass to the server?
- Ensure that the receiving player works on controlling with his feet, legs, chest and head to practice all controlling surfaces. Once they have mastered these, introduce both defenders closing down at once to put pressure on their control and make them think faster. The receiving player should be looking to be inventive and creative to both control the ball and make their pass.
- Swap the players around so that they all have a turn at being the receiver, server and defenders.

Skills practice

34. 1 v 1 – creating space (15–20 mins)

Set-up

Set up as a skills practice. The drill involves the Blue attacker against the Red defender and includes three servers.

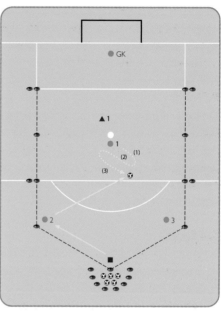

Drill flow

The Server takes a touch out of their feet and then plays the ball to Blue 2 or 3, who takes a touch and plays it to the feet of Blue 1. If Blue 1 needs to play it back to Blue 2 or 3, they can, but they must play it across to each other before playing it back to Blue 1. If Red 1 or the keeper wins the ball, can they play it to Blue 2 or 3 to reset the session?

Key factors

- Ensure the passing between the Blue players is crisp and solid and the ball into Blue 1 is to the feet. All players should be on their toes, playing with a high tempo and enthusiasm.
- The aim is to encourage the Blue player to find space to receive the ball, open up and attack the defender. He must work on his ability to 'pin' the defender and put him off balance, and then use this to create space.
- The trigger is the movement of the ball out of the server's feet. As soon as the Server touches the ball, Blue 1 moves up the pitch towards him (see (1)). As the server passes the ball to Blue 2, Blue 1 spins and moves with speed towards the goal (see (2)). As the ball reaches Blue 2, Blue 1 makes visual contact with him and checks back sharply to receive the ball (see (3)). This movement is a 'Z' run.
- On receiving the pass, Blue 1 should control the ball on the back foot and spin to face the defender. When he's in space, can he be positive and attack the defender? Does he have the space to dribble or run at the defender, or to strike at goal? Can he perform a turn or feint to create even more space? Ensure that Blue 1 does not simply perform a trick for trick's sake, but that all his movements are positive and lead towards the end product – a strike at goal.
- Once Blue 1 has mastered this skill, the other players take a turn.
- Progress to Blue 1 making a similar 'Z' run, but instead of controlling the ball, can he let it run and spin off to follow it? Can he work on a wall pass with either Blue 2 or 3, spinning around the defender to work his way through on goal?

attacker

Skills practice

35. 2 v 2 – creating space (20–25 mins)
Set-up
Set up as a skills practice. The drill involves working with two groups of two attackers and two defenders (eight players in total). The size of the area is 12m x 12m.

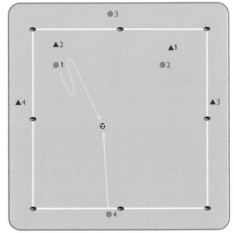

Drill flow
Two Blue players work against two Red players. The object is to make space and receive the ball from Blue 4 and then work the ball across the grid to Blue 3. If the Blue players achieve this, they keep possession and try and work the ball back. If the Red players intercept or win the ball, they play between the outside players, Red 3 and 4.

Key factors
- Ensure that the outside players are switched on and wait for the call to pass.
- Ensure the defenders defend realistically behind the attackers.
- Ensure that the attackers are working in the attacking third of the area, not the middle or defending area, as this will cut down on their space and limit their options.
- Both attackers should take their defenders high and wide to isolate them and generate 1 v 1 situations.
- The attackers should communicate with each other so that one player goes to receive the ball and the other stays high to isolate the defenders.
- The attacker that drops to meet the ball needs to make a 'Z' run (see p.91) to create space to receive the ball. Can they then receive on the back foot or half-turned and spin open to attack the defender?
- See above. Blue 1 made a 'Z' run to create space and receive the ball, Blue 2 has pinned his defender high to give Blue 1 a 1 v 1 situation. He now has the option to use a 'Z' run to create space for the pass, or hold Red 1 tight and receive a pass on his front foot to play a wall pass with Blue 1 to put him through.
- By creating space and 1 v 1 situations, the Blue players make it very difficult for the Red players to defend.
- Once the inside players have had a series of efforts, swap the inside players outside and vice versa to give all players a chance to attack.

Skills practice

36. Running at players – 1 v 1 progressing to 2 v 2 (20–25 mins)
Set-up
Set up as a skills practice. The drill involves working with two groups of two attackers and two defenders, using eight players in total. The size of the area is 12m x 12m.

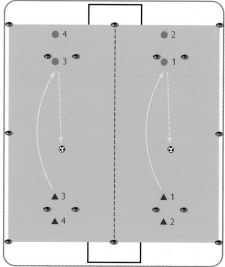

Drill flow
For each group the Red player plays the ball to the Blue player and then quickly closes him down. The Blue player controls the ball and runs at the Red player, looking to dribble around him and run with the ball through the two cones at the opposite end. If the Red player wins the ball, can he dribble through the cones at the Blue end? Once players have made attacks, join the two groups to make it 2 v 2 attacks on goal.

Key factors
- The passes to the attacker are high quality so that the topic can be coached properly.
- Ensure that the pass from the Red to the Blue players is of a high quality and direct to the player. Once the pass has been played, ensure the Blue player advances towards the pass and does not wait for it to arrive to him. By advancing towards the pass, the attacker is immediately putting the defender under pressure and dictating play to him, rather than the opposite.
- The attacker's first touch should be positive and out of his feet, allowing him to immediately start running with the ball, taking it a good distance. Ideally this first touch should be 1m away from the body.
- Can the attacker weight this first touch so that the defender feels they have a chance to get to the ball, but the attacker gets there first? With the defender committed, he should be able to touch the ball past him, or use a feint or turn to wrong-foot the defender.
- The attacker should meet the defender in at least the middle third of the area, if not the attacking third, which gives him space to be creative and to score.
- If the attacker needs to take extra touches to dribble at the defender, they need to either wrong-foot the defender and go past them, or work the ball to the side of the defender, using their body to shield the ball and make space for the pass or shot. Ensure that all turns and feints are positive and produce an end product (making space for a pass or shot) and are not just a trick.
- Once the players have attacked, remove the middle cones and enlarge the area for 2 v 2.
- Can the attacking players isolate defenders to make it 1 v 1, can they then offer angles for passes to make a 2 v 1 situation and can they produce the end product that is required, i.e. efforts at goal?

attacker

Technical practice

37. The technique of shooting (20–25 mins)
Set-up
Set up as a technical practice. The drill involves two players who work on their shooting skills, a keeper and two servers who each take a position in line with the edge of the six-yard box, just inside the penalty area or behind the players outside the penalty box.

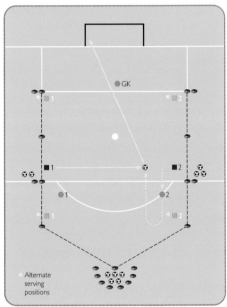

Drill flow
Blue 1 makes a run away from goal, turns quickly and calls for the pass from Sever 1. He plays the ball across Blue 1 who sets himself and then shoots first time at goal. Blue 2 repeats the process, receiving the pass from Server 2.

Key factors
- Ensure there is a fast tempo and balls are served in realistically.
- Ensure the players are relaxed and positive in their actions.
- Ensure the players' run back is sufficiently long to set themselves properly for the shot.
- During their run towards goal they must look up to see the position of the keeper, then look at the position where they want to place their shot and then look down and concentrate on the ball.
- They must ensure their head is steady and take small balancing steps prior to striking the ball to ensure they get their body in the correct position to take the shot.
- They should decide what type of shot to use based on the position of the player, the keeper and the ball.
- Ensure the players shoot at all times. If they cannot get an immediate strike at goal, allow them a touch, but they should concentrate on shooting first time.
- Swap players around regularly so they work on their least favourite shooting foot.
- Once all players have had their turn, introduce a defender who starts on the edge of the six-yard box and closes down the player passively (without tackling). Progress to add a second defender on the opposite side of the six-yard box with both defenders closing down simultaneously.
- Next time move the server's position, i.e. to the edge of the six-yard box so the players work on shooting with the ball arriving from a different angle.

Technical practice

38. The technique of shooting from close range (20–25 mins)
Set-up
Set up as a technical practice. The drill involves working with an attacker, two keepers and four servers. The size of the area is 12m x 12m.

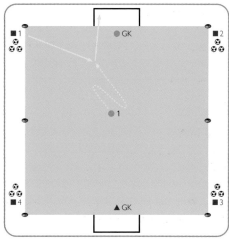

Drill flow
The attacker can call for a ball from any of the servers either by number, name, by pointing at them or visually. The ball is served in and he shoots at goal before resting to the middle and calling for another serve. The attacker can shoot at either of the goals.

Key factors
■ The passes to the attacker should be high quality so that the topic can be coached properly.
■ Work on the attacker's movement to receive the ball; it should never be direct. Instead, he should create space through a 'Z' run (see p.91) and look to meet the ball for a first-time shot.
■ The attacker should work on his levels of intensity, slow to set and make his initial move, then burst into activity to create space and get the shot.
■ Once he has created space he needs to assess the position and movement of the keeper. Can he take a look just prior to calling for the ball and decide on the type of finish to use? If possible, he should quickly glance to confirm his choice while the ball is being delivered and then concentrate on the ball to make the strike at goal.
■ Prior to striking the ball, the attacker should take several balancing steps to set himself.
■ Can he use different parts of his foot to shoot, deception to place the ball, power or finesse and, if possible, clever tricks to let the ball run, turning to finish?
■ After taking the shot, the attacker should be aware of rebounds from the woodwork or the keeper's save.
■ The coach should work with the player to discuss why shots are missed or saved, and the attacker should practise until he can regularly hit the target.
■ Ensure the servers challenge the attacker by playing balls in the air as well as on the ground.
■ Once the attacker has understood all the coaching points, progress to allowing the opposite server on the same side of the area to pressure once the call has been made, or alternatively put a defender next to the attacker to shadow the striker and try to intercept the passes.

attacker

Small-sided games

39. Shooting games (20–25 mins)
Set-up
Set up as a small-sided game. The Blue and Red teams have seven or eight players per team. They are set up with four or five players in their own half and two in the opposition's, plus the keeper. Goals should suit the age of the players.

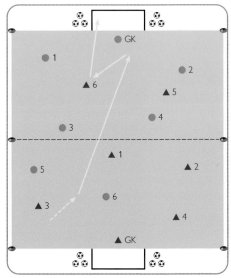

Drill flow
The ball starts with either keeper, who serves in the air or on the ground. Players look to shoot at the opposition goal, but must stay in their own half until swapped by the coach. The two players in the opposition's half cannot shoot directly, but should pressure the opposition players and follow up on any rebounds.

Key factors
- The players are looking to shoot at every opportunity, passing only when the shot is not on.
- Work on the attacker's movement to receive the ball. If marked, they should look to create space to receive the ball and find a shot (i.e. a 'Z' run, p.91).
- If players are marked and receive the ball, they can look for a pass, but ensure they take all shooting chances, from all angles.
- If a player receives the ball, can his first touch be out of his feet to free up his body for a shot? Can he then play with his head up to assess the position of the keeper before concentrating on the ball for his shot?
- Once he has looked at the ball, can he glance at where he wants to place the ball and then decide on the type of shot he will use? Will he curl the ball with the side of his foot, go for power with his laces, or chip it to the back post or over the keeper?
- Ensure players use their balancing steps prior to striking the ball so that they set themselves and get into the correct shooting position.
- Players in the opposition's half must look to move into an area where they can take any rebounds or secondary chances. They should work hard to apply pressure to the player looking to shoot.
- While the players in the opposition half cannot shoot themselves, they can be used for wall passes to set up the passer or another teammate for a shot from a different angle.
- See above. Red 3 has moved into a shooting position and made a shot, which is saved by the keeper. Red 6 has moved into a good position to place the rebound into the goal.

Functional practice

40. Shooting from in and around the penalty box (20–25 mins)
Set-up

Set up as a functional practice. The drill involves working with five overloaded attacking players against three defenders and the keeper, plus two servers and two targets (e.g. players, goals or cones). The size of the area is the width of the penalty area, to just in front of the halfway line.

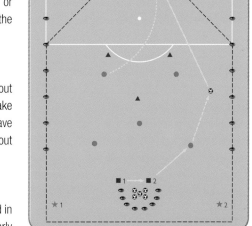

Drill flow

The ball is played from Server 1 to 2 and then out to any Blue player. The Blue players look to make space to shoot at goal. If the keeper makes a save or the Red defenders win the ball, can they play out with control to the targets?

Key factors

- Ensure there is a fast tempo, balls are served in realistically and that the players make early decisions and are positive.
- Everything must be directed towards striking at goal. Is their movement to create angles to receive the ball in good shooting positions? Can they receive the ball facing goal or half-turned so that a single touch allows them to face towards goal? Can they make runs to take them directly on to the ball to immediately strike at goal?
- Prior to striking the ball, do they take balancing steps to set themselves properly for the strike? Do they work on planting their standing foot in the correct position next to the ball for balance, so they get over the ball, keeping the shot on target?
- If the ball is in the air, do they adjust their body position for balance to get a clean and direct shot at goal?
- Ensure that when they get set to strike, the ball is back in their stance so they keep it low, and not forward where they will hit it high.
- Can they work on striking the ball across the back, middle and side to create swerve either in-to-out or out-to-in, or can they strike with their instep to give the ball swerve and dip?
- Can the players off the ball make movement to offer passing angles to set players up for strikes on goal? Can they make a 'Z' run (see p.91) to create space for their striker or for other players by dragging defenders away?
- Can the players nearest the goal react quickly to rebounds from the posts or off the keeper?
- Can attackers lay the ball backwards for teammates to strike the ball with swerve and bend, taking it around defenders, giving the keeper little time to react?

attacker

Functional practice

41. Beating the keeper when clear of the defence (20–25 mins)

Set-up

Set up as a functional practice. The drill involves working with four attackers playing against two defenders and the keeper, plus two servers and two targets (e.g. players, goals or cones). The size of the area is the width of the penalty area, to just in front of the halfway line. A line marked 18m from the edge of the penalty area marks the boundary across which the defenders cannot initially pass.

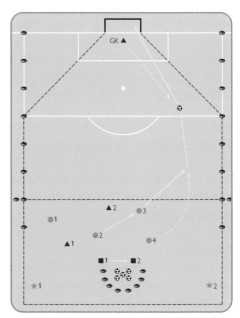

Drill flow

The ball is played from Server 1 to 2 and then out to any Blue player. The Blues look to make space and play the ball past the boundary line for the attackers to run at goal. Once past this line, the defenders relax, but another Blue player may follow up for rebounds. If the keeper makes a save or the Red defenders win the ball, can they play out with control to the targets?
Note: Where possible, use an assistant referee to challenge the timing of the runs from the attackers.

Key factors

- Ensure the defenders do not push up too high, which cramps the area and makes it difficult for the attackers to stay onside.
- Ensure the attacking players play at a fast tempo and look to isolate the defenders. Can they then play through balls to each other?
- Once the attacker is through on goal he must play with his head up to observe the keeper's position. Does he stay on his line? If yes, can the attacker use disguise to fool the keeper? Does he come off his line? Can he be chipped with a lofted shot or is it possible to dribble around him?
- Work on the striker's ability to go directly at goal and strike the ball in his stride pattern, which prevents the keeper setting his position.
- Prior to striking, does the player take balancing steps and focus on the ball if he is striking outside his stride pattern?
- If the player does miss or hit it straight at the keeper, explain why and get him to try again until he regularly hits the target.
- Do the other attackers follow up the run to pick up on any rebounds or saves off the keeper?
- Ensure that the Blue players rotate so that everyone gets a chance to attack at goal.

Functional practice

42. Attacking the far post and rebounds (20–25 mins)
Set-up
Set up as a functional practice. The drill involves working with four attackers playing against two defenders and the keeper, plus two servers and two targets (e.g. players, goals or cones). The size of the area is the width of the penalty area to just in front of the halfway line. A line marked 18m from the edge of the penalty area marks the boundary across which the defenders cannot initially pass.

Drill flow
The ball is played from Server 1 to 2 and then out to any Blue player. The Blues look to make space for themselves and play the ball past the boundary line for the attackers to run at goal. Once past this line, the defenders can relax, but another Blue player may follow up for rebounds. If the keeper makes a save or the Red defenders win the ball, can they play out with control to the targets? *Note:* Where possible, use an assistant referee to challenge the timing of the runs from the attackers.

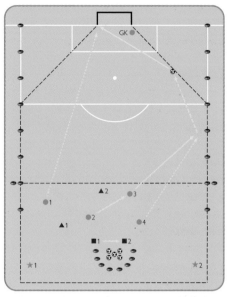

Key factors
- Ensure the defenders do not push up too high, which cramps the area and makes it difficult for the attackers to stay onside. All attacks at goal must be from wide angles.
- Ensure the attacking players play at a fast tempo and look to isolate the defenders. Can they then play through-balls to each other?
- Once the attacker is through on goal he must play with his head up to see the position and decision-making of the keeper. Does he stay on his line? If yes, can the attacker use a low shot with power aimed at the far post, or does the keeper come off his line and can he be chipped with a lofted shot to the far post?
- Can the attacker use a shot with the inside or outside of his foot to generate bend and send it around the keeper?
- As soon as the first attacker has made his run through on goal, ensure that the second attacker makes a run for the far post. During this run he must decide on the angle and timing; too early and the keeper parries the shot and the ball may bounce behind the second attacker. If he leaves his run too late, the shot may beat the keeper, but miss the far corner of the goal, going out of play, or the ball might hit the far post and rebound out or the keeper may make a secondary save.

attacker

Skills practice

43. Attacking techniques – 2 v 2 – crossovers (15–20 mins)
Set-up
Set up as a skills practice. The drill involves two Blue attackers against two Red defenders and also uses three servers.

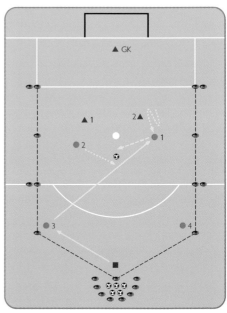

Drill flow
The Server takes a touch out of his feet and then plays the ball to Blue 3 or 4, who take a touch and play it to the feet of the furthest attacker. Blue 1 or 2 can play it back to the servers, but it must be played across before it can be played back. If the defenders or the keeper win the ball, can they play it to Blue 3 or 4 to reset the session?

Key factors
- Ensure the passing between the servers is crisp and solid and the ball into the attackers is to their feet.
- Ensure that the movement of the two Blue players pins the defenders square. To do this they need to drop towards the servers and then check back to put the defenders on the back foot, allowing them to receive the ball on the foot furthest away from the defender (receive on the front foot).
- The trigger to do this is the movement of the ball out of the server's feet. As soon as the server passes the ball to either Blue 3 or 4, the attackers move towards him. See above. As the ball reaches Blue 2, Blue 1 makes visual contact with Blue 3 and then checks back sharply towards goal, breaking to receive the ball (i.e. 'Z' run, p.91).
- As the pass is travelling to Blue 1, Blue 2 should be looking for Blue 1's first positive touch. As soon as this is made and Blue 1 has control of the ball, Blue 2 makes a run to the high side of 1 (the side that puts Blue 1 between Blue 2 and the defenders).
- As the players cross over, the player with the ball (Blue 1) communicates for the player without the ball (Blue 2) to either take or leave the ball. As soon as the move is performed, both players must spin and attack goal.
- The players need to work on calls to confuse the defenders or visual calls that let each other know what to do. At all times they need to be positive and work on achieving the end result, which is a strike on goal.

Skills practice

44. Attacking techniques – 2 v 2 – overlaps (15–20 mins)

Set-up

Set up as a skills practice. The drill involves working on two Blue attackers up against two Red defenders and also uses three servers.

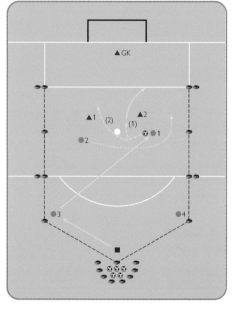

Drill flow

The Server takes a touch out of his feet and then plays the ball to Blue 3 or 4, who take a touch and play it to the feet of the furthest attacker. Blue 1 or 2 can play it back to the servers, but it must be played across before it can be played back. If the defenders or the keeper win the ball, can they play it to Blue 3 or 4 to reset the session?

Key factors

■ Ensure the passing between the servers is crisp and sold and the ball into the attackers is to their feet.

■ Ensure that the movement of the two Blue players pins the defenders square. To do this they need to drop towards the servers and then check back to put the defenders on the back foot, allowing them to receive the ball on the foot furthest away from the defender (receive on the front foot).

■ The trigger to do this is the movement of the ball out of the server's feet. As soon as the server passes the ball to either Blue 3 or 4, the attackers move towards him. See above. As the ball reaches Blue 3, Blue 1 makes visual contact with Blue 3 and then checks back sharply towards goal, breaking to receive the ball (i.e. 'Z' run, p.91).

■ As the pass travels to Blue 1, Blue 2 should look for Blue 1's first positive touch. As soon as this is made and Blue 1 has control of the ball and starts to open up, Blue 2 makes an arced run around and behind the high side of Blue 1. As Blue 2 is making this run, Blue 1 continues to open up and face the defender, looking for his reaction. If Red 1 holds the position, then Blue 1 can look to drive at Red 2 and play a ball behind him for Blue 2 to run on to (see (1)). If Red 1 tracks the run of Blue 2, then Blue 1 can continue to play left and attack the space that Red 1 has left.

■ If Blue 1 does attack goal, ensure Blue 2 looks to support a square pass from Blue 1 or any rebounds and secondary chances that may occur.

attacker

Skills practice

45. Attacking techniques – 2 v 2 – wall passes (15–20 mins)
Set-up

Set up as a skills practice. The drill involves working on two Blue attackers against two Red defenders and also uses three servers.

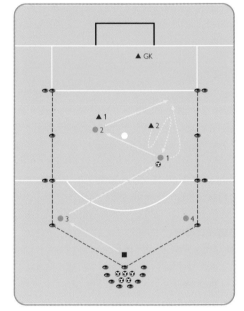

Drill flow

The Server takes a touch out of his feet and then plays the ball to Blue 3 or 4, who take a touch and play it to the feet of the furthest attacker. Blue 1 or 2 can play it back to the servers, but it must be played across before it can be played back. If the defenders or the keeper win the ball, can they play it to Blue 3 or 4 to reset the session?

Key factors

- Ensure the passing between the servers is crisp and solid and the ball into the attackers is to their feet.
- Ensure that the movement of the Blue player furthest from the server (Blue 1 here) uses the 'Z' run (see p.89) to pin the defender, and creates space to receive the ball on the back foot and spin open to face the defender.
- Blue 2 must stay deliberately deep to create a passing angle between the two attacking players and isolate the defender away from Blue 1.
- Once Blue 1 has made the turn, Blue 2 breaks towards 1 to offer a wall pass. Blue 1 then looks to pass into Blue 2's feet and make a run outside Red 2 to receive the pass back and shoot at goal.
- As soon as they have made the wall pass, Blue 2 needs to spin and look for rebounds or secondary chances to shoot at goal.
- If Blue 1 does not create space from the defender and is marked tightly, he can still look to use the outside of his foot to make a one-touch pass from the server to Blue 2 around the defender. Again, Blue 1 would then spin around the defender and attack goal.
- Blue 2 should also look to be creative, possibly faking a wall pass and letting the ball run past to spin out and follow the ball to attack goal.

Skills practice

46. Attacking techniques – 2 v 2 – diagonal runs (15–20 mins)

Set-up

Set up as a skills practice session. The drill involves working on two Blue attackers against two Red defenders and also uses three servers.

Drill flow

The Server takes a touch out of his feet and then plays the ball to Blue 3 or 4, who take a touch and play it to the feet of the furthest attacker. Blue 1 or 2 can play it back to the servers, but it must be played across before it can be played back. If the defenders or the keeper win the ball, can they play it to Blue 3 or 4 to reset the session?

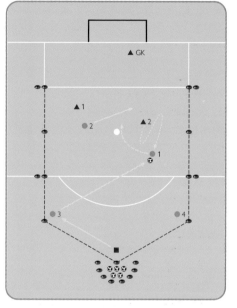

Key factors

- Ensure the passing between the servers is crisp and solid and the ball into the attackers is to their feet.
- Ensure that the movement of the Blue player furthest from the server (Blue 1 here) uses the 'Z' run (see p.89) to pin the defender, and creates space to receive the ball on the back foot and spin open to face the defender.
- Blue 2 must stay deliberately deep to create a passing angle between the two defenders and isolate them.
- Once Blue 1 has made a turn, Blue 2 makes a diagonal run across the six-yard box behind Blue 1's defender.
- If the defender Red 1 tracks Blue 2, Blue 1 can continue the run to the left and attack goal. If Red 1 holds position or starts to track across, reacting to Blue 1's run, he can play the ball through to Blue 2 to attack goal.
- If Blue 1 generates plenty of space, Blue 2 may decide to keep pinning Red 1 wide and leave the diagonal run late, looking to check wide and then breaking into the middle to receive a through ball from Blue 1 to attack goal.
- Depending on who attacks goal, the other striker should continue to attack goal and look to offer support for square passes or any rebounds and secondary chances.

attacker

Skills practice

47. Creating space to maintain possession 1 (15–20 mins)
Set-up
Set up as a skills practice. The drill involves working with five or six attackers and three defenders, plus a defending target player and a server. The size of the area is 12m x 12m.

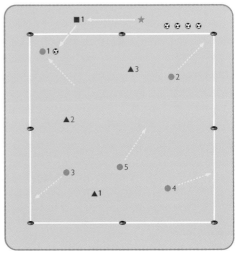

Drill flow
The defending Target player (blue star) plays the ball to the Server who then plays to a Blue player. The Blues work hard to maintain possession. Initially work on below head height passes and then progress to all types of pass. As this is a demanding exercise for the defenders, swap the target player and the server in for the defenders regularly.

Key factors
- Ensure players are switched on and play at a high tempo.
- Ensure that as the ball is played from the Target to Server 1, all the attackers move as wide as they can to split the defenders and create as much space as possible.
- Players need to work on their decision-making when looking for space so that they can offer for the Server's ball or create other passing options.
- Work on the players' body angle and stance. Ensure they are half-turned, so that they can see the server but also, with minimum head movement, they can see the rest of the playing area.
- Once the Blue player has possession, he then needs to work on his pass selection. Does he have space and can he use it to delay his pass, thereby committing a defender? Can he use disguise or feints to confuse the defenders or put them off balance?
- Once the pass is made, work on the players' movements. Do they simply pass and then stay in their own space or do they pass and then fill empty space to offer a return passing angle, moving and working the defenders?
- Can the players work in small units of twos and threes to create passing triangles and keep the ball moving with short passes?
- The key is the players' communication. Do they use both verbal and visual signals to work with their teammates to create space and let players know if they are open or not?
- Once the players have mastered the basics of the drill, allow them to pass beyond head height, but keep a check on their pass selection so that, if switching play, the receiver has time to control and keep possession.

Skills practice

48. Creating space to maintain possession 2 (15–20 mins)
Set-up
Set up as a skills practice session. The drill involves working with five attackers and five defenders, plus two neutral players (see striped triangles) and two Servers. The size of the area is 12m x 12m.

Drill flow
The Target plays the ball along the line and into a Blue player. Blue players work hard to maintain possession and can use the neutral players (N), who play for the team in possession. The team in possession can also use the Servers to maintain possession.

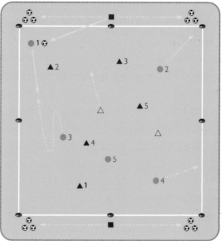

Key factors
- Ensure players are switched on and play at a high tempo.
- Ensure that as the Server plays the ball along the line, the Blue team, who are attacking first, move as wide as they can to split the defenders and create as much space as possible.
- Players need to work on their decision-making when looking for space so that they can offer for the Server's ball or create other passing options.
- Work on the players' body angle and stance. Ensure they are half-turned, so that they can see the server but also, with minimum head movement, they can see the rest of the playing area.
- Once the Blue player has possession, he then needs to work on his pass selection. Does he have space and can he use it to delay his pass, thereby committing a defender? Can he use disguise or feints to confuse the defenders or put them off balance?
- Once the pass is made, work on the players' movements. Do they simply pass and then stay in their own space or do they pass and then fill empty space to offer a return passing angle, moving and working the defenders?
- Can the players work in small units of twos and threes to create passing triangles and keep the ball moving with short passes?
- Work on the players' decision-making on when to play forwards quickly and when to slow play down to retain possession and draw defenders out. Once the players understand the key points of the drill set them goals such as making 10 passes to score a point. Once they have scored a point, they cannot score another until the opposition team has drawn level on points. Once they have made their 10 passes, do they then slow down to retain possession and frustrate the opposition?

attacker

Technical practice

49. Attacking heading principles (15–20 mins)
Set-up
Set up as a technical practice. The drill involves working with the Blue players in groups of two, three or four.

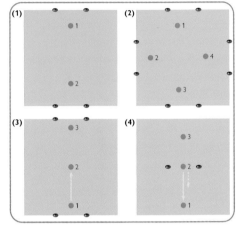

Heading from a standing position (see (1))
- As the throw-in occurs, ensure the player has his eyes firmly fixed on the ball and does not close them at the point he heads the ball. Work on then meeting the ball with the full forehead, just above the nose and below the hairline.
- Players need to generate power through their back, upper body and neck muscles. To help the players generate power, have them imagine that they have their arms on a bar in front of them. At the point of heading the ball, can they pull forwards on this bar and use their back, shoulder and neck muscles to generate full power?
- Can the players work on heading the ball down, trying to score past their partner by bouncing the ball past them into the goal?

Jumping to head the ball (see (1))
- As above, can they also judge the flight of the ball and move to get in line with it? As they jump, can they use their arms to generate more lift, allowing them to hang in the air? Can they head the top-middle of the ball to head it downwards towards the goal and again work on generating power through their arms?

Diving to head the ball (see (1))
- Players kneel down with their toes tucked under their legs. As the ball is served, can they drive forwards with their toes and legs to meet the throw? Their arms needs to be out in front of them to cushion their fall and they should head the ball in the centre to generate full power.

Glancing headers to change the direction (see (2))
- Players work in groups of four to score in any goal from the throw. Work on their body adjustment as the ball is thrown, early decisions on which goal they opt for and changing the direction of the ball with their body movement, and not their neck muscles.

Flicked headers (see (3))
- Players work in groups of three. Blue 1 throws to 2, who flicks the ball beyond and behind to 3, then they swap positions. The key is to get into the line of the ball, watch it on to the head, even as they drop their chin to their chest, and then with a quick flick, play it up and over the keeper.

Looped headers (see (4))
- Blue 2 throws to 1 and then closes him down. Blue 2 loops his header up and over 1 to try and score. Blue 3 retrieves the ball and 1 goes into goal. Work on adjusting to the flight of the ball and heading below the middle with the top of the forehead. Power is generated from the legs, waist and torso.

Skills practice

50. 2 v 2 – attacking heading (15–20 mins)

Set-up

Set up as a skils practice. The drill involves working with two attackers and two defenders. The size of the area is 12m x 12m.

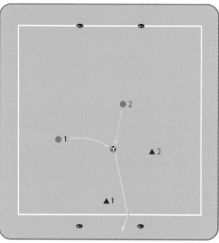

Drill flow

The Blue team starts with the ball. Blue 1 throws the ball to 2 who tries to score in the Red goal. Once they have had their effort at goal, the Red team follow the same procedure. Get players to throw different sorts of passes, i.e. high for a jumping header, low for a diving, short for a glancing header, lobbed for a flick on etc.

Key factors

- As the throw occurs, ensure the player has their eyes firmly fixed on the ball and does not close them at the point they head it. Work on them meeting the ball with the full forehead, just above the nose and below the hairline.
- Players need to generate power through their back, upper body and neck muscles. To help the players generate power, have them imagine that they have their arms on a bar in front of them. At the point of heading the ball, can they pull forwards on this bar and use their back, shoulder and neck muscles to generate full power?
- Can the players work on heading the ball down, trying to score past the defender by bouncing the ball past them into the goal?
- Ensure that the players use good movement to create space for the header and don't simply stand still, waiting for the ball to arrive. Can they make runs at the goal so that it is realistic to a game situation?
- When they get into position and the throw is made, check for the correct body stance and body shape to make the header. Work with the player to ensure this is correct.
- Work with the player on their decision-making and the type of header they use. Do they stand to head when they should have jumped? In a game the defender may beat them to the ball.
- If the player misses the head, work with them to understand why – was it the wrong choice of header? Was their technique wrong or did they need to work to create more space and hence time? Should they have been nearer to goal? Did they head it at ground or straight at a defender etc?
- Ensure that the players are always positive in attacking goal and hitting the target.

attacker

Small-sided game

51. Attacking heading (20–25 mins)
Set-up
Set up as a small-sided game. The drill involves working with one team on their attacking heading technique and attacking structure. Teams should ideally contain seven or eight players.

Drill flow
Teams start in the structured start position. The team being coached **do not** start with the ball; players throw, head and catch the ball in that sequence. See opposite. Blue 4 throws the ball to Blue 6 who heads it for Blue 5 to catch. If the ball touches the ground, it is lost and opposing players cannot catch the ball. If they head it they win possession, even if the other team catches the ball.

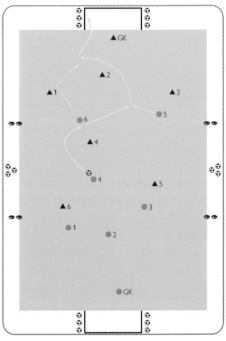

Key factors
- Ensure that play is at a high tempo and that defensively the teams maintain a realistic structure and shape.
- As a coach, you are looking to observe what happens when the ball is won and how the players react.
- As soon as the ball is won, do players around the thrower move to create space and support the thrower?
- Once the ball is worked into the attacking third, do the front players make runs towards the goal so that they have scoring opportunities, or do they use clever runs to split defenders?
- When a player is marked, does he time his run to take him across the defender and get into a position where he can meet the ball first?
- Give tactical instructions ('go long', 'drop short', '1–2' etc) so that both the thrower and potential catcher know what the player intends to do.
- Can the players play with their heads up? Can the catcher be aware of dangerous runs into the opposition's area so he can deliver the ball quickly?
- The keeper must communicate clearly and concisely to ensure the team keeps its shape and that they do not all rush off to attack, and risk losing shape in case possession is lost.

Phase of play

52. Developing play from the goalkeeper's possession
Set-up

Set up as a phase of play. The drill involves working on the defending team and how they play out from the back once they regain the ball. It involves the keeper, a back four and midfield four. The opposition comprises the midfield four and two strikers, plus a target player.

Drill flow

The Blue team start with the ball and play it directly to the target player, who then plays it into one of the attacking Red midfielders. They play and attack goal as directly as possible. Once the Blue team regains possession, particularly the keeper, can they play with control to the Target? If the ball goes out of play, normal rules apply, but corners are not awarded.

Key factors

- Ensure there is a fast tempo and the attacking team try to play balls beyond the defence so that the topic can be coached.
- Work on the decision-making of the keeper once they have possession, and the movement of the players in front of the keeper to get into good positions to receive the ball.
- Can the two full backs drop to receive the ball with their body stance open and facing up the pitch to see who the keeper or defenders are closing them down? If one of the fullbacks receives the ball, can either or both of the centre backs drop to offer another passing angle, should the fullback not be able to pass upfield through the midfielders?
- When the keeper has the ball, can a central midfielder drop to create space to receive the ball and then look to open up and play forwards?
- See above. The ball has been played behind the defence and the keeper has collected it. Blue RB drops to receive the ball and faces up the pitch. The attacking Red LM makes an arced run to deny the pass up the wing, so Blue RB 'recycles' the ball through the Blue CBR, who drops to give a good passing angle. He then plays it across field to Blue RB, who drops to collect the ball. The marker Red RM is not as quick to close down and Blue LB makes his pass upfield to Blue LM who plays with control to the target. Repeat the session.
- Work on the keeper's decision-making. Can he release play quickly upfield with a quality throw, or short-kick to a player such as a wide midfielder, centre midfielder or striker? Does he hold the ball and play with control?
- Ensure players share information quickly and clearly.

attacker

Small-sided game

53. Transition from defending to attacking (20–25 mins)
Set-up
Set up as a small-sided game. The drill involves working with the Blue team on making the transition from defending to attacking once they regain possession. Teams should contain seven or eight players.

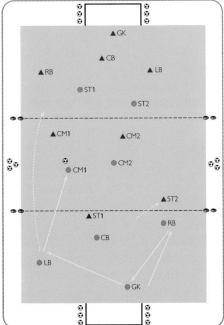

Drill flow
Teams start in the structured start position. The Red team start with the ball. Let the drill flow for several phases to settle players. Once possession has been won, introduce the coaching points. If the ball goes out of play, normal rules apply, but corners are not awarded.

Key factors
- Ensure play and team structure is realistic and played at a high tempo.
- You are aiming to establish patterns of play that will allow the Blue team to build from the back once the ball is won, achieving entries into the attacking third of the pitch.
- Ensure that all players play with their heads up and are comfortable on the ball.
- Ensure the defenders work as a unit to build play from the back. Don't let them force play – they should be confident to recycle the ball to probe for openings in the midfield or to play quickly to the attacking front players.
- The defenders must be aware of their position and the risk associated with losing the ball. This must not force them into playing long balls, but rather ensure they pick the right pass.
- The midfield players must work hard to isolate their markers from the ball to create passing angles to receive. If the marker tracks them, they have created space for the player on the ball; if they let them go, they have created space to receive.
- The two front players must not simply hold their positions, which makes them easy to mark, but should take up an attacking position where they can see the ball, the goal, their marker and their support players or striking partner.
- See above. The keeper plays the ball to Blue RB, however, Red ST2 makes a good run to cut off his forward movement so he recycles the ball back through the keeper. The keeper sees that Blue LB has dropped and is free so passes to him. Blue LB makes a quick pass into Blue CM1's feet. Blue LB makes a strong overlap run past Blue CM1, who now has several choices. Does he play the ball back to Blue LB or into the feet of one of his strikers? Either way, he must look to drop and cover Blue LB to give balance to the team should the ball be lost.

Small-sided game

54. Quick counter-attacking from deep positions (20–25 mins)

Set-up
Set up as a small-sided game. The drill involves working on one team to counter-attack quickly once possession has been regained. Teams should contain seven or eight players.

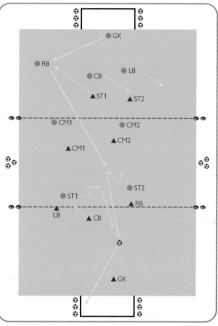

Drill flow
Teams begin in the structured start position and the Red team starts with the ball. Let the drill flow for several phases to settle players. Once possession has been won, introduce the coaching points. If the ball goes out of play, normal rules apply, but corners are not awarded.

Key factors
■ Ensure play and team structure is realistic and played at a high tempo.

■ This drill is ideal if the team has practised dropping off and defending with a compact shape once the ball is lost (see pp. 84 or 86).

■ The furthest striker should hold a high line on the shoulder of the last defender to offer a quick outlet once the ball is won.

■ When possession is regained, the player with the ball must play with his head up to see the options available. If he can play quickly to a high midfielder or striker, he should do so.

■ Ideally the ball should be played either into an area of poor defence that the high striker can attack or directly to the high striker.

■ See above. The defending centre back and left back have broken wide left to make space for the defending right back to receive the ball from the keeper. Blue ST2 has made an out-in-out run to create space and receive the ball to his feet from Red RB. Blue ST1 has made an in-out-in run to move Red CB left and create space to his receive the ball from his strike partner for a shot at goal.

■ The supporting players should work hard to get up the field and support the striker with the ball, but ensure they maintain a defensive shape.

■ Ensure the keeper communicates to the defence to push out and hold a high line and keep their shape once his team is on the attack.

■ Good interplay between the two strikers is essential to try and move defenders to make space for their strike partner, or to make their own space to receive the ball.

■ The strikers should be positive. As soon as a shooting opportunity arises, they should attack goal. The second striker should be sure to follow up for any rebounds.

attacker

Small-sided game

55. Counter-attacking – quick movement to support and finish (20–25 mins)

Set-up

Set up as a small-sided game. The drill involves working on one team to counter-attack quickly once possession has been regained and players' reactions to support each other. Teams should contain seven or eight players and both the pitch and goals should suit the age of the players.

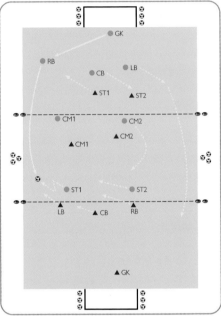

Drill flow

Teams begin in the structured start position and the Red team starts with the ball. Let the drill flow for several phases to settle players. Once possession has been won, introduce the coaching points. If the ball goes out of play, normal rules apply, but corners are not awarded.

Key factors

- Ensure play and team structure is realistic and played at a high tempo.
- The coach needs to convey that players should know when to play with a high tempo and when to relax and build with a controlled structure. If the ball is won deep in their defending half and the opportunity exists to break quickly, this should be done at speed and with purpose. If this opportunity doesn't exist, the team should relax and build from the back.
- If the team is counter-attacking quickly, individual players should react with runs into space or areas that are poorly marked. Can they move across or behind defenders to isolate them and create 1 v 1 situations? Can they make runs that take defenders away and create space for the player on the ball or others to receive the ball? If the ball is played up to a front target player, can they react quickly to support him? Can they make 'Z' runs (see p.91) to create space to receive?
- Can players work in units to create counter-attacking opportunities? See above. Blue CB and LB have broken wide to move the two strikers, creating space for Blue RB. He has played a quick ball to Blue ST1 who has made space with a 'Z' run. Blue ST2 has also broken to the same side to draw the defenders across, creating space behind. Blue LB has exploited this by making a strong run into this space to support the strikers. Blue CM2 has spun around his defender to offer a passing angle. Blue CB and LB worked as a unit to create space for Blue RB and Blue ST1 and 2 worked together to create space for Blue LB. To maintain shape, Blue CM1 must drop to cover Blue LB.
- If the ball does not find its way to Blue LB, players must understand that these runs make space for others and that they have to be unselfish and positive in making them.

Phase of play

56. Running with the ball (20–25 mins)
Set-up
Set up as a phase of play. The drill involves working on the attacking team's ability to create space for the player with the ball to make runs at the opposition. The drill comprises two strikers, four midfielders and two fullbacks. Opposition comprises the keeper and back four, plus the two central midfielders and one of their strikers, plus two servers and two targets (e.g. players, portable goals or cones).

Drill flow
The ball is played from Server 1 to 2 and then out wide to Blue RM or LM, or Blue LB or RB. Let the play run for several phases to observe how the players react. If the ball goes out of play, normal rules apply, but corners are not awarded.

Key factors
- Ensure that play is realistic with the defenders and midfielders pushed up the pitch.
- The aim is to work on patterns of play from different unit groups of players. Can these players work for each other to move defenders and create space for the player in possession to make runs with the ball?
- See above (1). The ball is played wide to Blue RM who has created space using a 'Z' run – (see p.91) and received the ball on the back foot and turned to see the defender in front of him and his support players. He has two choices: he can run at Red LB and using a turn, feint or dribbling skills, take him on and beat him out wide to then deliver a cross. Or he could run at his inside and, depending on the run of Blue ST2, he can either look for a through ball to a striker or, if he can get close enough, have a strike at goal. If Blue ST2 breaks to his right and the defender follows, the shot will be on. If the defender holds, he could play a ball through to his striker.
- See above (2). The ball has been played to Blue LB and, due to the run of Blue CM1, which has moved Red CM1, Blue CM2 now has space to receive the ball and make a strong run at the defence. Depending on the movement of the players in front, he may get a strike at goal or make a through-ball pass.
- It is important that all players play with their heads up and understand that their movement affects the game, either creating space for the player in possession, or putting them in space to receive.

attacker

Phase of play

57. Creating space in the middle third (20–25 mins)
Set-up

Set up as a phase of play. The drill involves working on the attacking team's ability to create space for the player with the ball to make runs at the opposition. The drill comprises two strikers, four midfielders and two full backs. Opposition comprises the keeper and back four, plus the two central midfielders and one of their strikers, plus two servers and two targets (e.g. players, portable goals or cones).

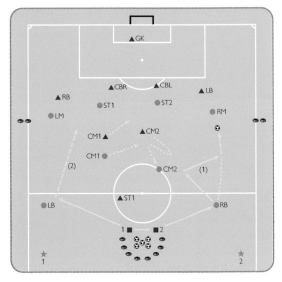

Drill flow

Ball is played from Server 1 to 2 and then out wide to Blue RM or LM, or Blue LB or RB. Let the play run for several phases to observe how the players react. If the ball goes out of play, normal rules apply, but corners are not awarded.

Key factors

- Ensure that play is realistic with the defenders and midfielders pushed up the pitch.
- The aim is to work on patterns of play from different unit groups of players. Can these players work for each other to move defenders and create space in the middle third for the player in possession to make runs with the ball?
- See above (1). The ball is played wide to Blue RB who then looks for a wall pass from Blue CM2 who has pinned Red CM2 and created space for Blue RB to attack using a 'Z' run (see p.91). Blue RB can now look to link with either Blue RM or play to the strikers to generate an effort on goal.
- See above (2). The ball has been played to Blue LB, and due to the run of Blue CM1, which has moved Red CM1, he now has space to make a strong run at the defence. Depending on the movement of the players in front he may get a strike at goal or make a through-ball pass.
- Once the space has been created in the central midfield area, it is important that the players work hard to generate an end product; this can be more entries into the attacking third, and further crosses, efforts at goal or goals.

Small-sided game

58. Changing the direction of play (20–25 mins)

Set-up

Set up as a small-sided game. The drill involves working on one team to change the direction once possession has been regained and players' reactions to support each other. Teams should ideally contain seven or eight players.

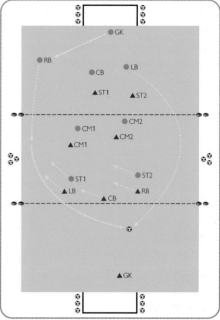

Drill flow

Teams begin in the structured start position. The Red team starts with the ball. Let the drill flow for several phases to settle players. Once possession has been won, introduce the coaching points. If the ball goes out of play, normal rules apply, but no corners are awarded.

Key factors

- Ensure play and team structure is realistic and played at a high tempo.
- The aim is to work on patterns of play from different unit groups of players. Can these players work for each other to move defenders and create space to play in?
- Players should play with their heads up and vision. Can they see the movement of other players, especially their teammates, and how they are moving defenders to expose areas of weakness or make areas that are poorly defended?
- Can the ball be moved from areas that are heavily defended to create opportunities to break, generating goal-scoring opportunities?
- The types of play that should be used to switch play are cross-field diagonal balls triggered by forward player runs, overlap runs (see p.101) triggered by good possession, and supporting player runs to either receive the ball or act as a decoy to move a defender. Also use crossover runs (see p.100) triggered by good possession and the clever run of a supporting player, or clever and creative play such as back heels, flicks or reverse passes to confuse defenders and attack areas of weakness.
- All require other players to move defenders with runs and calls, so that the player with the ball can play into the space.
- See above. Both Blue strikers have made runs towards the ball and dragged their defenders with them. Seeing the space created, Blue LB makes a strong run down the left side and Blue RB is able to send a long diagonal ball across to them.
- Work on the above patterns of play with key units of players so that they understand and begin to see patterns and can react to them.

attacker

Small-sided game

59. Forward runs without the ball (20–25 mins)
Set-up
Set up as a small-sided game. The drill involves working with one team on forward runs by players without the ball and players' reactions to support each other. Teams should ideally contain seven or eight players.

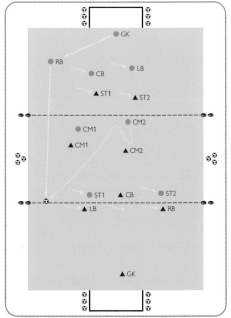

Drill flow
Teams begin in the structured start position. The Red team starts with the ball. Let the drill flow for several phases to settle players. Once possession has been won, introduce the coaching points. If the ball goes out of play, normal rules apply, but no corners are awarded.

Key factors
- Ensure play and team structure is realistic and played at a high tempo.
- The key aim is to work on the forward runs of players without the ball into areas of space created by their teammates or to areas that are poorly defended.
- Players should understand how their run affects the opposition and the shape of their team.
- Players can either make runs to draw defenders away and create space behind them, to exploit space or to make runs into poorly defended areas.
- The type of runs that can be used are overlap runs (see p.101) or diagonal runs (see p.103). Can they make space to receive the ball or draw players away with a 'Z' run (see p.89)? Can they check towards the ball and break away to draw a defender out, or can they make a run from the inside of the pitch wide, or a run inside from wide on the pitch to move defenders?
- If a player is behind the ball and can see the space or a poorly defended area, can he use diagonal runs into this space or an overlap run to get in front of the ball and offer a passing angle?
- If the player is in front of the ball and can see the space or a poorly defended area, can he make well-timed runs across the defender to receive the ball, i.e. a near- or far-post run? Can he make a 'Z' run to create space, allowing him to receive the ball on the back foot, turn out and attack goal, or can he get on the blind side of his defender and move wide to accept a cross-field pass?
- See above. Blue CB and LB move left to draw the two strikers away. The keeper passes to Blue RB, and the two strikers move quickly right to draw the defenders away. Seeing the run of the two strikers, Blue CM2 pins Red CM2, puts him off balance and makes a forward run to the right. Rather than running with the ball and giving the opposition time to reorganise, Blue RB plays a quick ball into the space. Blue CM2 attacks the goal. Both strikers should spin and attack goal, looking for rebounds and secondary chances.

60. Movement to create and exploit space (20–25 mins)
Set-up
Set up as a small-sided game. The drill involves working with one team on movement to create and exploit space. Teams should ideally contain seven or eight players.

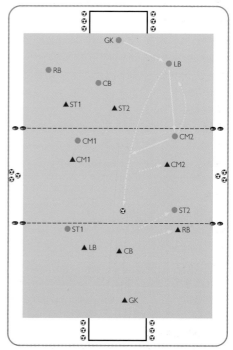

Drill flow
Teams start in the structured start position, Blue team with the ball. Let the drill flow to settle players. Once possession is won, introduce the coaching points. If the ball goes out of play, normal rules apply, but corners are not awarded.

Key factors
- Ensure play is realistic and at a high tempo.
- Work on players' movement and reactions once the ball is regained. Do they move early into position to create space throughout the team?
- If space is created in the defending third, players must be careful not to lose their shape in case the ball is lost. If space is created in the middle third, the midfield must be mindful of the actions of their partner. If one attacks, does the other hold to give the team balance and screen the opposition strikers?
- The forward players should ensure that one of them is in a position to offer themselves as an outlet player. If they receive the ball, they must be able to hold the ball or attack goal.
- Communication starts with the keeper ensuring the defenders offer passing angles, but are also mindful of their shape. The defenders communicate to the midfield to maintain balance and the midfield should communicate to the strikers to ensure they are creating space and offering outlets.
- All players must keep their heads up to see their teammates' movement and make the best decisions. If players are tightly marked, can they use the 'Z' run (see p.91) to create space or to pin and unbalance the defender to then make their run into space?
- Can players receive the ball on the back foot and half-turned to see the players in front of them, the ball and the defenders nearest them and to play forwards quickly or attack goal?
- Can the player on the ball play the ball into space for their teammate to run on to?
- The type of runs the players need to make to create space are runs from the middle of the pitch, wide, runs from wide to the middle, crossover runs, overlap runs and diagonal runs (see pp. 100–103)
- See above. Blue LB receives the ball and plays it to Blue CM2 who has made an inside-to-out run. Blue LB runs into the space created by Blue CM2 and receives a wall pass (see p.102) from him. He runs with the ball at the defence. Blue LB can either shoot at goal or look for a strike partner.

attacker

Small-sided game

61. Forward passes to the player or to space (20–25 mins)
Set-up

Set up as a small-sided game. The drill involves working with one team on their decision-making on whether to play to the player or to space. Teams should ideally contain seven or eight players.

Drill flow

Teams start in the structured start position, Blue team with the ball. Let the drill flow to settle players. Once possession has been won, introduce the coaching points. If the ball goes out of play, normal rules apply, but corners are not awarded.

Key factors

- Ensure play is realistic and at a high tempo.
- Work on players' movement and reactions once the ball is regained. Do they move early into position to create space throughout the team?
- It won't always be possible for the ball to be played quickly forwards as the opposition have reacted quickly to losing possession and taken up good defensive positions.

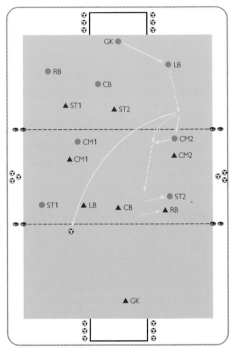

- Communication starts from the keeper ensuring the defenders offer passing angles, but remain mindful of their shape. The defenders communicate to the midfield, to maintain balance and the midfield to the strikers to ensure they are creating space and offering outlets.
- If players are tightly marked, can they use the 'Z' run (see p.91) to create space or to pin and unbalance the defender to then make their run into space?
- Can players receive the ball on the back foot and half-turned to see the players in front of them, the ball and the defenders nearest them and to play forwards quickly or attack goal?
- Work on the decision-making of the player in possession. Is there room to play a cross-field, diagonal or up-the-line ball into space behind the last opposition defender? Can they play the ball directly to the highest striker's feet? Can they play into a teammate's feet and look for a wall pass (see p.102) or will they be forcing a pass, and should they recycle the ball so that they can attack from a different angle?
- Blue LB receives the ball from the keeper and runs with it to the edge of the defending third. Blue CM2 has made an in-to-out run to drag his marker wide and Blue ST2 has too pulling the opposition defenders wide. Red LB has been caught ball-watching and Blue ST1 has worked to his blind side. Seeing this, Blue LB makes a forward pass into the space behind the defence. If Red CB sees the danger and drops to cut off this pass, Blue LB could look to play a wall pass with Blue CM2 and then travel with the ball to link up with the strikers.

Functional practice

62. Wide midfielders' movement to create and exploit space (20–25 mins)

Set-up

Set up as a functional practice. The practice involves two strikers, two central midfielders and the wide midfielder and fullback from the same side. Opposition is the goalkeeper, three defenders and two centre midfielders.

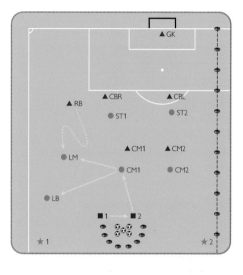

Drill flow

The ball is played from Server 1 to 2 and then into the Blue CM1 who plays it wide to either Blue LM or LB. Let the play run for several phases to see how the players react. If the ball goes out of play, normal rules apply, but corners are not awarded.

Key factors

- Ensure that the defenders (Reds) are pushed up to a realistic position and defend realistically.
- The aim is to work on the movement and runs of both Blue wide flank players. Where possible the ball should be played through the central midfield players and then out to wide players.
- Blue CM1 and 2 should look to create space to receive the ball, or try to get their markers tight so that they can flick the ball wide and pin the defending central midfielders.
- When working on the wide Blue LM to create space, the players must master their 'Z' run (see p.91) to create the space to receive the ball on their back foot and spin to face the defender.
- Once they have created this space, received the ball and turned, they need to play with their head up to see the options. Can they run at the Red RB and use their pace to take the defender on the outside, or use feints, turns or dribbles to beat them and deliver the cross? They may also look to drive towards Blue ST1, and as the fullback Red RB closes, play a wall pass to get in behind him and deliver the cross.
- If the wide midfielder cannot make space and is tightly marked, can they hold the ball and look for the run of Blue LB? If the defending fullback stays tight to Blue LM, can he lay the ball off for Blue LB to take and drive into space? If Red RB makes a movement to follow Blue LB, can Blue LM use this space to spin and see the options available?
- At all times the attacking fullback, Blue LB, should look to overlap Blue LM where possible as this will produce 2 v 1 situations.
- Both wide players must be mindful of what the end product is – a cross shot at goal or dragging the ball back to an approaching teammate.

attacker

Functional practice

63. Roles and responsibilities of a wide player (20–25 mins)

Set-up

Set up as a functional practice. The practice involves two strikers, two central midfielders and the wide midfielders and fullbacks, the opposition is the goalkeeper, back four and two centre midfielders.

Drill flow

The ball is played from Server 1 to 2 and then in to the Blue CM1, who plays it wide to the wide midfielders or the fullbacks. Let the play run for several phases to see how the players react. If the ball goes out of play, normal rules apply, but corners are not awarded.

Key factors

- Red defenders are pushed up, with only one responding fullback attacking while the other holds.
- The aim is to work on the movement and positioning of all Blue wide flank players. When they have possession, can the two wide midfielders hold wide to stretch the defence and create space in the middle?
- Blue CM1 and CM2 should create space to receive the ball and play it wide to one of the wide midfielders, or if they cannot lose their markers, get them tight so that they can flick the ball wide and pin the defending central midfielders.
- Use the 'Z' run (see p.91) to create space to receive the ball on the back foot and spin to face the defender.
- Once they have created space, received the ball and turned, they need to play with head up. Can they be really positive and run at the defending fullbacks, using their pace to take the defender on the outside, or use feints, turns or dribbles to beat them and deliver the cross? They may also drive towards the nearest attacker to see how the fullbacks react. If they close, can they play a wall pass to get in behind them and deliver the cross? If they hold, can they get a shot at goal?
- If the wide midfielder cannot make space and is tightly marked, can they hold the ball and look for the fullback's supporting run on their side? If the defending fullback stays tight, can they lay the ball off for the fullback to take and drive into space or to deliver a deep cross?
- If wide players can deliver a cross, where does it need to go, what sort of cross should it be, how do they react afterwards, cover, follow-up etc?
- The wide player should see if he can make positive runs into the box towards the far post.
- If possession is lost, the wide midfielders should react quickly to ensure the opposition is unable to counter-attack. Assess how to contain the opposing fullback, if they need to tuck in and compact play, if their fullback has gone beyond them and they need to drop and cover his position.

Functional practice

64. How to deliver the cross (20–25 mins)

Set-up

Set up as a functional practice. The practice involves two strikers, two central midfielders and the wide midfielder and fullback from the same side. The opposition is the goalkeeper, three defenders and two centre midfielders.

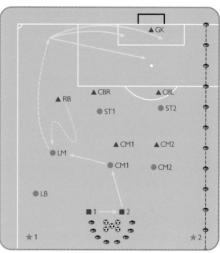

Drill flow

The ball is played from Server 1 to 2 and then into Blue CM1, who plays it wide to Blue LM or LB. Let the play run for several phases to see how the players react. If the ball goes out of play, normal rules apply, but corners are not awarded.

Key factors

- Red defenders are pushed up, with one responding fullback attacking while the other holds.
- The aim is to improve the crossing technique of the two wide players, so they should look to deliver a cross at every opportunity.
- Blue CM1 and 2 should create space to receive the ball, or try and get their markers tight so that they can flick the ball wide and pin the defending central midfielders.
- Use the 'Z' run (see p.91) to create space to receive the ball on the back foot and spin to face the defender.
- Once they have created this space, received the ball and turned, they need to play with their head up. Can they run at the Red RB and use their pace to take the defender on the outside, or use feints, turns or dribbles to beat them and deliver the cross?
- If the wide midfielder cannot make space and is tightly marked, can he hold the ball and look for the run of Blue LB? If the defending fullback stays tight to Blue LM, can he lay the ball off for Blue LB to take and drive into space wide past Red RB?
- Blue LB should overlap Blue LM where possible, which produces 2 v 1 situations with the defending fullback.
- Before crossing the ball, the player needs to play with their head up and decide the type of cross they will deliver and to where. If it is to the near post, will it be along the ground at pace, cut back to be hit, drifted in to be headed, or whipped across the front of the six-yard box with swerve to get around a player? If it is to the far post, will it be with pace and bend or lofted to hang for a striker to attack?
- Prior to striking the ball, can they take small balancing steps to set themselves? When they strike the ball can they use the side of the foot and the ankle to send in a cross with power and swerve? Can they strike the ball with different parts of the foot for a different cross, such as a chip or a lofted ball?
- If it is not possible to get to the byline for the cross or the defender closes the player down, can they play backwards for a deeper cross from the fullback?

attacker

Phase of play

65. Scoring from crosses (20–25 mins)
Set-up
Set up as a phase of play practice. The practice involves two strikers, two central midfielders and the wide midfielders and fullbacks. The opposition is the goalkeeper, back four, two centre midfielders and a retreating striker.

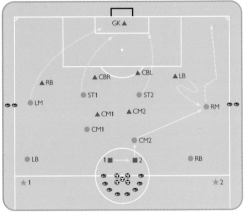

Drill flow
The ball is played from Server 1 to 2 and then into Blue CM2, who plays it wide to Blue RM or LM. If the ball goes out of play, normal rules apply, but corners are not awarded.

Key factors
- Red defenders are pushed up, with one responding fullback attacking while the other holds.
- The aim is to work on finishing from crosses.
- Blue CM1 and CM2 should create space to receive the ball and as soon as possible play the ball wide with quality to one of the wide midfielders. The players must master their 'Z' run (see p.91) to create the space to receive the ball on their back foot and spin to face the defender.
- They should look to beat the fullback down the line to deliver the cross. (Ask the fullback to let the player go and put limited pressure on the wide midfielder so that you can get quality crosses into the box. The wide midfielder must cross in on the run and at speed to help the attacking players work on the timing of their runs).
- Work on the movement of the attacking players to get into key areas, the midfielders to make late runs into the area to pick up deeper crosses or to attack the far post, and the opposite wide player to attack the back of the six-yard box.
- If attacking the near post, the player needs to run across the defender to get in front of him to meet the ball. They must time their run to arrive just as the ball does. To finish, they may look for a flicked header either up and over the keeper or down at the ground, or a glancing header up and over the keeper to the far post. Alternatively, they may look to meet the ball with a side-footed shot which they should leave late to give the keeper minimal reaction time.
- If attacking the middle of the goal, the player makes a run across the defender to get in front of him to meet the ball, or checks to create space. Either way, they must time their run or movement to arrive just as the ball does. To finish they may look for a jumping header to a corner or down to beat the keeper, a diving header or a volley. If they have time, can they control the ball for the finish?
- If attacking the far post they must time their run to arrive just as the ball does. To finish, they may look for a jumping header with power to a corner or they could loop the ball back across goal to the far post. Alternatively, they could meet the ball with a driven volley or side-footed finish.

Small-sided game

66. Attacking the goal from crosses (20–25 mins)
Set-up
Set up as a small-sided game. The practice involves the goalkeeper and six or seven teammates, against an opposing team of the same make-up. Two channels are marked 6–9m in from the side lines for the two target players (playing for the side that has possession) to play in. The area is full-pitch width by 36m deep.

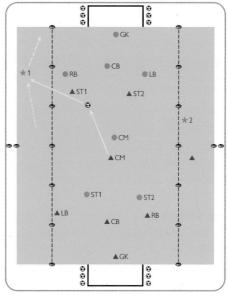

Drill flow
Teams begin in the structured start position and the Red team starts with the ball. Let the drill flow for several phases to settle players. Once possession has been won, introduce the coaching points. If the ball goes out of play, normal rules apply, but no corners are awarded.

Key factors
- Ensure that play and the team's shape is realistic.
- The aim is to work on the attacking players' movement to get into key areas and the midfielder's movement to make late runs into the area to pick up deeper crosses or attack the far post.
- If attacking the near post, the player should make a run across the defender to get in front of him to meet the ball. They must time their run to arrive just as the ball does. To finish, they may need to look for a flicked header either up and over the keeper or down at the ground, or a glancing header up and over the keeper to the far post. Alternatively, they may meet the ball with a side-footed shot, which they should leave late to give the keeper minimal reaction time.
- If attacking the middle of the goal, the player makes a run across the defender to get in front of him to meet the ball, or checks to create space. Either way, they must time their run or movement to arrive just as the ball does. To finish they may look for a jumping header with power to a corner or down to beat the keeper, a diving header or a volley. If they have time, can they control the ball and steady for the finish?
- If attacking the far post they must time their run to arrive just as the ball does. To finish, they may look for a jumping header with power to a corner or they could loop the ball back across goal to the far post. Alternatively, they could meet the ball with a driven volley or side-footed finish. Can they control the ball and steady for the finish?
- Ensure you pick two target players that can deliver a quality cross ideally off their left or right foot. If they prefer one foot, get them to work on their weaker foot to deliver, but also allow them to cut back and send in crosses with the stronger feet so the attackers can practise their finishing skills.

attacker

Small-sided game

67. Support in attack (20–25 mins)
Set-up
Set up as a small-sided game. The drill involves working with one team on their decision-making on how to support each other in the final third. Teams should ideally contain seven or eight players.

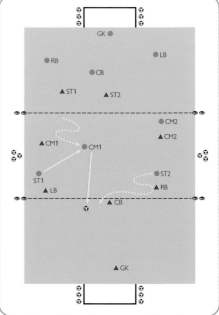

Drill flow
Teams begin in the structured start position and the Red team starts with the ball. Let the drill flow for several phases to settle players. Once possession has been won, introduce the coaching points. If the ball goes out of play, normal rules apply, but no corners are awarded.

Key factors
- Ensure that play and the team's shape is realistic.
- Work on the players' decision-making on the distance and angle of their support. This will very much depend on the ability and creativity of the player involved. If the player on the ball is full of tricks and turns, the support may want to keep their distance to either avoid being drawn close to the player, or they may naturally close this player down and therefore generate support player's space.
- If support players are supporting from behind the ball, can they take up positions that give them a full view of the field before them? Can they create space to receive the ball comfortably without pressure? Can they use this time and space to play the ball forwards into space for players to run on to, or play the ball into the feet of the forward players. If the opportunity allows, can they change the direction of the attack?
- If they cannot find space and receive the ball under pressure, can they play backwards or sideways to maintain possession and recycle the ball, building from the back with a different direction of attack?
- If the player is offering support play from in front of the ball towards goal, can they create space using the 'Z' run, or can they create space for the pass, breaking to get on the ball?
- See above. The ball is played into the Blue ST1's feet, but he has his back to the defender and is tightly marked. Blue CM1 uses the 'Z' run to create space for a pass and offer support and Blue ST2, who had initially taken the player wide, also uses a 'Z' run to pin the defender and runs across the front of the CB. Blue CM1, seeing the movement of Blue ST2, plays a ball through to and in on goal. If Red CB reacts to Blue ST2's run and moves left to cover it, Blue CM1 is then able to drive at goal and potentially get a shot on target.

Phase of play

68. Creating and exploiting space in the final third (20–25 mins)
Set-up

Set up as a phase of play. The practice involves two strikers, two central midfielders, the wide midfielders and fullbacks. The opposition is the goalkeeper, back four, two centre midfielders and a retreating striker.

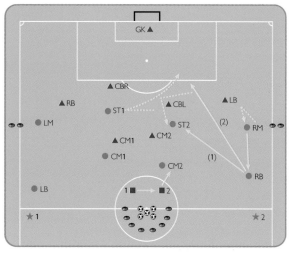

Drill flow

The ball is played from Server 1 to 2 and then into the central midfielders or directly to the wide midfielders, who then look to play forwards. Let the play run for several phases to observe how the players react. If the ball goes out of play, normal rules apply, but corners are not awarded.

Key factors

- Ensure the Red defenders are pushed up to a realistic position, and that only one fullback is attacking while the other holds a realistic position.
- The aim is to work on the movement of the two attacking players to create holes in the defence for either of them to exploit. Both players must be aware of where their playing partner is and develop an understanding of when the other will react, i.e. to look for and understand their triggers.
- The ball is played out to the wide Blue RM, however, they haven't lost their defender and so send the ball back to Blue RB. As the ball is played back, the nearest striker, Blue ST2, runs across their defender and breaks back to look for the ball. Blue RB has two options: (1), he plays the ball into Blue ST2's feet and if he has time, receives on the back foot and turns to open out and looks to play forwards, or (2), he plays a through ball between the defending fullback and centre back, but this needs Blue ST1 to have reacted to the run of Blue ST2 and for them to spin out and break into this gap.
- If, when the ball is played to the wide midfielder, they are able to create space and turn, then they are looking for the runs of the two strikers and the opposite wide midfielder who, if the left defending fullback is ball-watching, may be able to get on their blind side and attack the far post.
- Can the two central midfielders create space down the middle by dragging their defenders wide and allowing either server to play a direct ball to one of the attackers, who must open out and watch the movement of their striker partner and the two wide fullbacks?

attacker

Phase of play

69. Movement, receiving and turning in the final third
Set-up

Set up as a phase of play practice session. The practice involves two strikers, two central midfielders and the wide midfielders and fullbacks. The opposition is the goalkeeper, back four and two centre midfielders and a retreating striker.

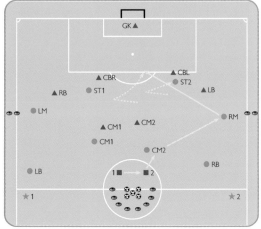

Drill flow

The ball is played from Server 1 to 2 and then into the central midfielders or directly to the wide midfields, who then look to play forwards. Let the play run for several phases to see how the players react. If the ball goes out of play, normal rules apply, but corners are not awarded.

Key factors

- Red defenders are pushed up, with one responding fullback attacking while the other holds.
- The aim is to work on the movement of the two attacking players to create holes in the defence for either of them to exploit. Both players must be aware of where their playing partner is and develop an understanding of when the other will react, i.e. to look for and understand their triggers.
- If the ball is played out to the wide midfielder, can Blue ST2 draw his defender across the pitch towards ST1 and then spin out to break the other way for the defender to follow? At the same time ST1 should check inside-to-out to drag his defender across, but as he sees ST2 make his break, he can spin and break through the hole created by ST2 and receive the ball from Blue RM to shoot at goal. If Red CBL does not follow ST2, Blue RM can slide the ball down the line for him shoot.
- Alternatively, ST2 can hold his line, pinning the defender, and then drop back down the pitch slightly to receive the ball on his front foot with the defender behind. Can he use a turn, such as a step-over to his left, and using the outside of his right foot, knock the ball sideways? With the defender off balance, can he slide to ST1 or take a shot himself?
- Another option when the ball is wide is to use the 'Z' run (see p.91) to create space. If so, can he slide in his attacking partner, or look to play the wide midfielder in behind the defending fullback?
- Can the players look for creative play? If the wide midfielder plays the ball in, can the closest attacker feint control and then dummy the ball, letting it run to his partner? Upon making the dummy, can he spin out, running to receive a flicked return ball or create space for his partner to shoot?
- The key is to get the two attacking strikers to work together on patterns of play that should become natural to them.

Phase of play

70. Combination play to finish (20–25 mins)
Set-up
Set up as a phase of play. The practice involves two strikers, two central midfielders, the wide midfielders and fullbacks. The opposition is the goalkeeper, back four, two centre midfielders and a retreating striker.

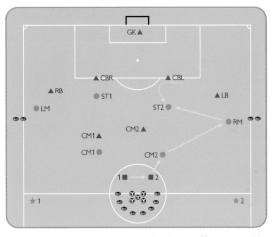

Drill flow
The ball is played from Server 1 to 2 and then into the central midfielders or directly to the wide midfields, who play forwards. Let the play run for several phases to observe player's reactions. If the ball goes out of play, normal rules apply, but corners are not awarded.

Key factors
- Red defenders are pushed up, with one responding fullback attacking while the other holds.
- The aim is to work on the movement of the two attacking players, who use all 2 v 2 attacking skills learned in sessions 43–6. They should play with their heads up, and be aware of each other's, the support players' and the defenders' positions.
- See above. Blue ST2 moves across the defender to pin him and drops to create space and receive the ball on the back foot, turning to face the defender. He must choose his pass based on the defender's movement. If the defender marking ST2 has followed and created a 'saw tooth' shape in the defensive line, can he play a wall pass (see p.102) to ST1 and run around Red CBL to have a shot at goal? If the defender has kept shape can ST2 make a run towards the middle of the two centre backs and look for a diagonal run (see p.103) from ST1? If the centre backs still hold, can he play ST1 through? If Red CBR follows, can he shift left and strike at goal? Can the strikers play a crossover (see p.100), where ST2 allows ST1 to take the ball? Or do they perform a 'fake take', where ST2 keeps the ball and looks for another pass or a shot? Players can also use overlaps, back heels, feints and turns to beat players.
- If the ball is with the attacking fullback, and it is played into either striker, can they look to dummy, letting the ball run to their strike partner and spinning to receive or create space?
- The coach should encourage the players to take all goal-scoring opportunities. Players must not get into the habit of over-complicating things – if the chance is there to shoot, SHOOT!

set pieces

Principles of defending set pieces

The session plans below look at the three main methods of defending set pieces, which are:

1 Man to man marking.

2 Zone marking.

3 A mixture of zone and man to man marking.

Principles

Common themes run through all three ways of defending:

- From where are goals scored? Can we defend these areas?
- Can we limit efforts outside this area to headers so these are easier to deal with?
- Until the ball is played nobody can score, therefore each defender must remain focused and know their role.
- By reducing the options available you limit the chances to score, therefore work on getting the first touch away to safety with a header.
- Any shots in and around the danger area can go over, possibly around, but never through the defenders.
- Remember; only one person can score, therefore isolate the threat and deal with it.

Organisation

- Who? Who does what and where? These decisions should be made on factors that include the player's height, determination to win the ball and their level of aggression or bravery.
- Where? Identify the danger zones, such as the near post, central area, far post, and edge of the box, and the areas of secondary defending, such as outside the box or the back of the penalty area.
- When? Set early, be aware of quick corners and then reassess as the ball comes in.
- How? Reduce the danger by blocking runners and heading the ball clear.
- Why? Identify the danger zones, the danger attackers and the delivery of the ball.
- Role? Ensure the players know their roles – is it marking space, an attacking player, the near or far post, or being an outlet for counter-attacking?

Technical details

- **Body shape**. The player's body shape must be open so they can see the ball and the attacking players (i.e. defending triangle, p.91). Ensure players don't ball-watch!
- **Front foot**. Ensure the players are on their front foot and are ready to attack the rectangle or zone in front of them
- **Angle and distance**. Work on the players' positioning – how far do you want them from each other? Could an attacking player slip into that space? Work on how far out the players marking a zone are from the goal and each other. Do they cover all the spaces? Is the keeper confident in covering the space inside the zones to deal with the threat of balls between these players and the goal?

- **Clearance**. Can the players clear with width, height and distance?
- **Secondary responsibilities**. Who has to deal with any secondary balls? If you have players on the posts, when do they leave them? How do you counter-attack and when do you want the team to push up?

Mental qualities

- Ensure the players understand the key qualities they must have, such as discipline, concentration, alertness, composure, determination (bravery), the ability to read the delivery, anticipation and movement.
- As you deliver the session, ensure you build on these qualities with the players and that each player knows their responsibility before you continue to the next coaching point.

The following three session plans are only guides and you may well need to adapt them to suit your own players, based on the points above.

set pieces

Functional practice

71. Defending corners – zone marking (20–25 mins)

Set-up

Set up as a functional practice. The practice involves the entire Blue team defending against corners sent in by either one or two Red attacking players.

Drill flow

The Red player crosses in the ball and the Blue team works on clearing it to safety. Either work with one group of players such as the keeper and players Blue 2–7 to ensure they have understood their roles before introducing Blue 8–11, or work with the entire defending team. Progress by introducing attacking players.

Key factors

- Ensure crosses are of a high standard and that the attacking players attack the goal in a realistic way.

- See above. Blue 2 and 3 mark the posts. Blue 3 must be aware that his role is also to deal with any threats at the back post, so his body shape must be such that he can see the threat and the ball.

- Blue 11 can either take up a position to prevent an unobstructed cross and make the attacker put more height on the ball, thereby giving the keeper more time to deal with the cross, or he can position himself near the halfway line, which usually forces the defending team to leave two players back to cover him. If Blue 11 does position himself near the corner, and if the attacker crosses an in-swinging ball, then the defender should be further from the goal line. If the cross is an out-swinging ball, then he should be on or just off the line. Once the ball has gone over Blue 11, he can work on his counter-attacking roles and responsibilities, but he should also be aware that a high percentage of clearances might come back into the area he is covering. Finally, if the attacking team plays a short corner, Blue 11 is the player to pressure them.

- The team's best headers of the ball should take up the positions of Blue 5, 6 and 7, and Blue 4 (he may be the smallest of the four players). Their role is to attack the ball and clear to safety with the head.

- Blue 8–10 take up positions between Blue 5–7, but towards the edge of the area for compactness. Their role is to both clear the ball with headers and block attackers' forward runs.

- The keeper should expect to claim the ball in the red shaded area (see above). If the keeper does call for the ball, then it is the responsibility of all other defending players to block runners and protect him (especially important for Blue 5–7).

Functional practice

72. Defending corners – man for man marking (20–25 mins)
Set-up
Set up as a functional practice. The practice involves the entire Blue team defending against corners sent in by either one or two Red attacking players.

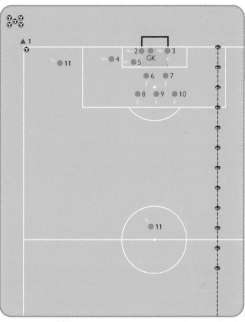

Drill flow
The Red player crosses in the ball and the Blue team works on clearing it to safety. Either work with one group of players such as the keeper and players Blue 2–7 to ensure they have understood their roles before introducing Blue 8–11, or work with the entire defending team. Progress by introducing attacking players.

Key factors
- Ensure crosses are of a high standard and that the attacking players attack the goal in a realistic way.
- See above. Blue 2 and 3 mark the posts. Blue 3 must be aware that his role is also to deal with any threats at the back post, so his body shape must be such that he can see the threat and the ball.
- Blue 11 can either take up a position to prevent an unobstructed cross and make the attacker put more height on the ball, thereby giving the keeper more time to deal with the cross, or position himself near the halfway line, which usually forces the defending team to leave two players back to cover him. If Blue 11 does position himself near the corner, and if the attacker crosses an in-swinging ball, the defender should be further from the goal line. If the cross is an out-swinging ball, then he should be on or just off the line. Once the ball has gone over Blue 11, he can work on his counter-attacking roles and responsibilities, but he should also be aware that a high percentage of clearances might come back into the area he is covering. Finally, if the attacking team plays a short corner, Blue 11 is the player to pressure them.
- The team's best headers of the ball should take up the positions of Blue 4 and 5 to deal with any in-swinging corners.
- Blue 6–10 take up positions to man-mark, block runners and clear the ball, preferably with headers. When blocking, can they keep their arms out and put their body in line with the attacker's run towards the goal or ball?
- The coach decides if they want the man-marking players watching the ball and the player or just the player (depending on players' heading qualities).
- The keeper should expect to claim the ball in the red shaded area (see above). If he does call for the ball, it is the other defending players' responsibility to block runners and protect him (especially important for Blue 5–7).

set pieces

Functional practice

73. Defending corners – combined zones and man for man (20–25 mins)

Set-up

Set up as a functional practice. The practice involves the entire Blue team defending against corners sent in by either one or two Red attacking players.

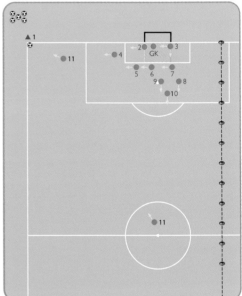

Drill flow

The Red player crosses the ball in and the Blue team works on clearing it to safety. Either work with one group of players such as the keeper and players Blue 2–7 to ensure they have understood their roles before introducing Blue 8–11, or work with the entire defending team. Progress by introducing attacking players.

Key factors

- Ensure crosses are of a high standard and that the attacking players attack the goal in a realistic way.

- See above. Blue 2 and 3 mark the posts. Blue 3's role is also to deal with threats at the back post, so he must position himself to see the threat and the ball.

- Blue 11 can either take up a position to prevent an unobstructed cross forcing the attacker to put more height on the ball, thereby giving the keeper more time to deal with the cross, or position himself near the halfway line, which usually forces the defending team to leave two players back to cover him. If Blue 11 does position himself near the corner, and if the attacker crosses an in-swinging ball, the defender should be further from the goal line. If the cross is an out-swinging ball, then he should be on or just off the line. Once the ball has gone over Blue 11, he can work on his counter-attacking roles and responsibilities, but he should also be aware that a high percentage of clearances might come back into his area. Finally, if the attacking team plays a short corner, Blue 11 should pressure them.

- The team's best ball headers should take up the positions of Blue 5, 6 and 7, and Blue 4 (he may be the smallest of the four players). Their role is to attack the ball and head to safety.

- Blue 8–10 take up positions to man-mark, block runners and head the ball clear. When blocking, can they keep their arms out and put their body in line with the attacker's run towards the goal or ball?

- The coach decides if they want the man-marking players watching the ball and the player or just the player (depending on players' heading qualities).

- The keeper should expect to claim the ball in the red shaded area (see above). If he does call for the ball, it is the other defending players' responsibility to block runners and protect him (especially important for Blue 5–7).

Functional practice

74. Attacking corners (20–25 mins)
Set-up
Set up as a functional practice. The practice involves the attacking team attacking the goal from corners. Use eight attackers, plus a defending keeper. The goals and area should be relevant to the age of the players.

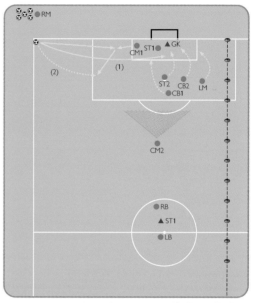

Drill flow
The Blue attacking player crosses the ball in and the Blue team works on getting attempts on target. Either work with one group of players such as the crosser, near-post attacker and the attacker blocking the keeper before introducing the other players, or with the entire attacking unit. Progress by introducing defending players.

Key factors
■ Ensure crosses are of a high standard and that the attacking players attack the goal in a realistic way.
■ The key is to ensure that players know their start positions and responsibilities, and for the attacking players to react to the flight of the ball.
■ See above. Blue ST1 positions himself tight to the keeper to be a nuisance and, once the cross is made, to look to latch on to any loose balls and shoot at goal. Blue CM1 looks to start on the near post and break towards the ball, to look for flick-ons or, if time allows, get a touch and a shot at goal.
■ The two centre backs and second striker (or your three best headers of the ball) look to group up on the back post towards the back of the penalty box. On the crosser's signal or trigger movement, the three players look to attack the back post, middle of goal and front-middle of goal.
■ Blue LM looks to position himself at the back of the six-yard box for over-hit crosses, or flicked on, half-cleared balls to either head back into the box or strike at goal themselves.
■ Blue CM2 takes up a position outside the box and looks to either play any balls cleared forwards back into the box, or strike at goal.
■ The two fullbacks should mark the striker if one is left upfield. If two or more remain, the coach must make a decision on how many and whom he wishes to drop. If three defending players are left upfield, the suggestion would be to match them in numbers.
■ All attacking players should be positive, attack the ball with their heads, and time their runs to arrive at the ball, judging its flight.
■ In option (2), Blue CM1 breaks to the ball and plays a wall pass back to Blue RM who then crosses or shoots at goal depending on the reaction of the defenders – again work out a call for this.

set pieces

Functional practice

75. Defending set pieces (20–25 mins)
Set-up
Set up as a functional practice. The practice involves the whole team defending against free kicks from central and wide positions near the defending goal.

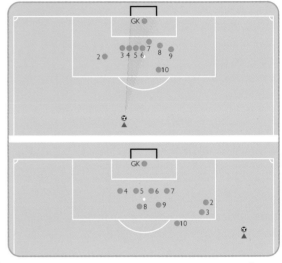

Drill flow
Attacking players strike the ball at goal or cross it in and the defending team work on clearing the ball to safety. Progress by introducing attacking players.

Key factors
- For central attacking free kicks, consider the following: is the free kick direct or indirect? Who is taking the free kick – are they left or right-footed, will they bend or go for power? Defensively, how many players will be in the wall and who will call this (ideally it should be the keeper)? Where do we want our tallest players, in the middle of the wall or on the ends to guard the posts? Will someone charge the ball? Who will it be – someone from the wall, or from the side of the wall? What are the positions of the players outside the wall; will they mark zones or man to man? Can the wall stay in line, and not turn their backs or close their eyes? Can they step forwards and stand on tiptoe to make them tall, while preventing a shot underneath? What is the keeper's start position – can he see the ball? Are defenders in the way? Once the strike is taken, can the defenders turn quickly for rebounds? Can players react to clever play if the ball is chipped behind or played backwards or sideways?
- Once a free kick has been awarded, can the nearest player get in front of the ball to prevent a quick kick? A defender and the keeper decide how many are in the wall and where they stand. Blue 4 is on the right post and Blue 3 stops curled shots to this side. Blue 2 stops any clever passes down the side, charging the ball if required, as does Blue 10. Blue 7 protects the left-hand post in case the shot is driven and the rest of the defenders zone mark the attackers. The keeper should be just off centre so that he can react to either side.
- Defending free kicks from wide positions is similar to defending corners (see pp. 129–131) and as a coach you must decide if you will zone mark, man for man mark or combine both. Once a free kick has been awarded, can the nearest player get in front of the ball to prevent a quick kick? For wide free kicks two players need to be in the wall. Blue 2's position is in line with the near post to prevent drilled shots. Blue 4–7 should be the best ball headers and start far enough away from the goal so that, should an attacker get a touch, the keeper has time to deal with it, but close enough that a cleverly timed run from an attacker does not give them space to clear the defence and get a shot. Other players man mark and act as blockers. The keeper should start so that he can defend both front and back posts. Blue 10 defends the edge of the area and launches counter-attacks if the ball is won. If the ball is cleared, can the team get back into its normal shape quickly?

Functional practice

76. Attacking set pieces (20–25 mins)

Set-up

Set up as a functional practice. The practice involves selected attackers against the remaining players, who act as defenders.

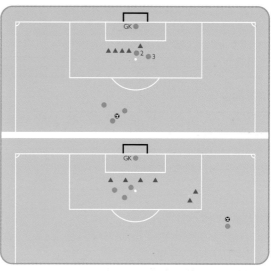

Drill flow

Work on different methods of attacking the goal from both central and wide free kicks. Either work with one group of players, such as the free-kick takers, or with the whole attacking unit. Use either defending players or, if you have them available, mannequins to make the defending wall.

Key factors

- Ensure the defensive wall is realistic to fully challenge the attacking players.

- For attacking free kicks, consider the following before the free kick is taken: is it direct or indirect? Is it to the left, right or central to the goal? Who have the opposition put in their wall and how many? How switched on are the defenders? Has the referee told the attacking team to wait for the whistle? How far is the free kick from goal? Once all these factors have been assessed, the attacking team need to decide who will take the free kick and whether they go for goal. You may want to try and confuse the opposition with clever free-kick routines, or you might ask one person to go for goal and have the others follow up and look for rebounds.

- For a central free kick, have an assigned left-footed player and right-footed player who will take the kicks and a back-up in case either are off the pitch. Can you assign the role of joining the wall to two players to try and block the keeper's line of sight and to confuse the wall and other defenders? If the free-kick taker is going to attack goal, do you need to send up your centre backs?

- In the central free-kick example three players are at the ball. If the free kick is indirect, can one touch the ball and a second strike? If it is direct, can they decide between them and two join the wall? Can one break wide for a sideways pass to change the angle and avoid the wall?

- For wide free kicks, have a left and a right-footed player on the ball. Do they want an in-swinging free kick, or an out-swinging free kick? Can the two centre backs be brought up to attack the ball in a similar way to attacking corners (see p.132) along with a third so that the front, middle and back of goal can be attacked?

- Once you have assigned the free-kick roles, set the takers homework to practise their technique. Assess them over three to four weeks.

set pieces

Functional practice

77. Defending throw-ins (20–25 mins)
Set-up
Set up as a functional practice. The practice involves working on the defending team to defend throw-ins. Use six defenders, and four attackers.

Drill flow
The ball is thrown in, short or long. Can the defending team react quickly to get into position and defend the threat? Once the ball is won, can it be played with control to a target (i.e. a player, goal or cones)?

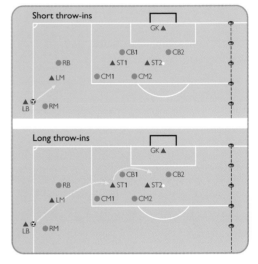

Key factors
- Ensure the throws are of a high quality and in accordance with the rules.
- Ensure that the attacking team plays with realism to challenge the defenders.
- Ensure the defenders move into position quickly when the ball is being retrieved or collected and not when the attacking team is about to throw it in.
- For short throws, ensure the defenders mark tightly in and around the ball and that someone pressures the thrower once he has put the ball back into play. Can the defenders put heavy pressure on the attacker's first touch and make him play with his head down?
- For long throws, have one player in front and one behind the attacking target player. Ensure that the defenders are at least matched size for size with the attacker or ideally taller.
- For the majority of flick-ons the average distance achieved will be 2–6m, so can the next defender be positioned to deal with the secondary ball?
- The keeper should take up a position nearer to the front post than the back, as the ball is unlikely to carry beyond this position.
- Players need to concentrate to understand the opposition's tactics. If the right back takes the throws most of the time, can they understand his maximum distance? If they bring in a specialist long ball thrower, can they adapt to meet this threat? Work on body shape, the defensive triangle (see p.68) and front screening (see p.70).

Functional practice

78. Attacking throw-ins (20–25 mins)
Set-up

Set up as a functional practice. The practice involves working on the attacking team to create space and chances from their throw-ins. It involves five attackers, four defenders and the keeper.

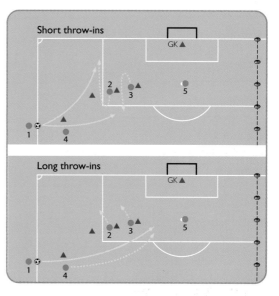

Drill flow

The ball is thrown in from different positions in the attacking third. Can the attacking team create space to deliver the cross or get a shot off at goal? If the ball is won, can the defending team play it with control to a target (i.e. a player, a goal or cones)?

Key factors

▪ Ensure the throws are of a high quality and in accordance with the rules.

▪ Ensure that the defending team plays with realism to challenge the attackers.

▪ The attacker who is taking the throw has two choices when he throws the ball – does he throw to feet or to space? In terms of the options of who to throw to, he can throw down the line to Blue 2, to the edge of the area for Blue 3 or over the top to Blue 4.

▪ Blue 2 and 3 must make runs in the opposite direction to each other and then check back to lose their markers.

▪ Once they have lost their markers and received the ball, can they either deliver the cross or get a shot off at goal?

▪ Blue 2 and 3 must time their runs to ensure they go at the same time and when the thrower is ready.

▪ If the throw is to be long, can Blue 2 and 3 make a run towards the byline to take the defenders away and create space for Blue 4 to run into? If the throw is long, can Blue 4 either head the ball on for the striker, or control the ball and get a strike on target?

fitness conditioning

Technical practice

79. Basic fitness session (time varies depending on age/ability)

The following fitness sessions can be used individually or grouped in an extended fitness session. This will depend on how, as a coach, you want to condition your players. You can also give these sessions to the players as homework and ask them to carry out the session themselves or with a playing partner/s.

Fartlek (around soccer pitch)

3 or 4 laps as fast as possible

1 lap walk recovery

2 laps jog with 10m sprint at each corner

1 lap walk recovery

3 x lengths of the pitch sprints with walk back recovery

Fitness circuits

After each exercise, sprint 20m and then jog 20m.

Press ups x 12

Squats x 12

Sit ups x 12

Star jumps x 12

Lunge x 12

Squat thrusts x 12

5 min walk recovery

Pyramid sprints

20m sprint, walk back

30m sprint, walk back

40m sprint, walk back

50m sprint, walk back

60m sprint, walk back

50m sprint, walk back

40m sprint, walk back

30m sprint, walk back

20m sprint, walk back

Interval (around soccer pitch)

1 lap fast; 1 lap slow;

½ lap fast; ½ lap slow.

Repeat 3 times.

Fig. 06:01 Fitness circuits

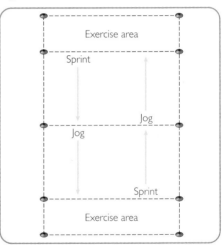

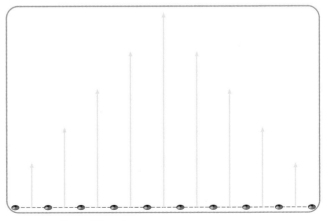

Fig. 06:02 Pyramid sprints

Technical practice

80. Ball skills fitness training (time varies depending on age/ability)

To ensure your players work on their fitness, but don't tire of the tedium of constant running, vary the sessions so that you include a ball and make it fun.

(A) Touch and move

Work in groups of four in as many grids as required. Three Blue players work the Red player in the middle. Two Blue players have a ball, and one does not. The Blues take turns to play the ball to Red, who must pass to the Blue player without a ball. Start with passes on the ground and let each player in the grid have a turn, then move on to bouncing the ball, where the Red player must catch it before it bounces. Finish and move on to headers. Ensure the three Blue players keep moving and work the player in the middle hard.

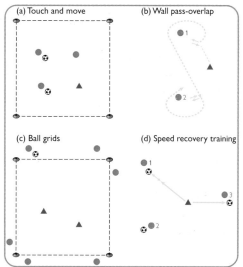

Fig. 06:03 Ball skills

(B) Wall pass-overlap

Each player should have a turn as Red, performing six repetitions each. Red sprints to Blue 1 who plays a wall pass to him. Red sprints around Blue 1 and down to Blue 2, who then gives a wall pass to Red. He then sprints around Blue 2 and back to the start. Continue this circuit for 45–60 seconds.

(C) Ball grids

Six Blue players start on the outside and two Red players in the middle. The Reds have to try and win the ball by intercepting the Blues' passes. The Blues have to pass it through the grid to another player. Add conditions such as a minimum of two touches, one touch, following the pass or their own variety. Work the Reds for 45–60 seconds and then swap around. Each player should work in the middle three times.

(D) Speed recovery training

Players work in groups of four, three Blue players and one Red working in the middle. The three Blues space out around the Red player, approximately 15m apart. Red sprints to a player, calls for a pass, plays it back to the Blue player and then sprints back to the middle. The Blues then take it in turns to make the calls and Red sprints to them, plays a wall pass and returns to the middle. Work for 45–60 seconds, each player having a go to complete a set. Repeat the complete set five to six times.

fitness conditioning

Technical practice

81. Speed and agility (time varies depending on age/ability)
Agility and reaction drill

Players line up one behind the other between cones set 15m apart. The coach stands facing them and calls left, right, forwards or back and the players must mimic the calls. Progress to arm pointing only to ensure the players are moving with their heads up. Work the players constantly for 60–90 seconds, repeating three to five times.

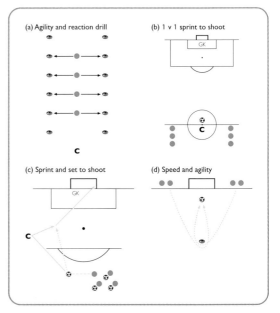

1 v 1 sprint to shoot

Players line up in pairs on the halfway line (or a third of the way up the pitch, dependent on the players' age and ability). The coach plays a ball towards the goal (the pass must be with some pace to reach towards the edge of the penalty area). As soon as the pass is made, the two players sprint towards the ball. The winning player must take a touch out of their feet and strike at goal. Ensure they use maximum effort to win the race to the ball. Vary it by making the players lie on their bellies, kneel, face backwards and go on the coach's call or use your own variations to mix up the drill.

Sprint and set to shoot

Players line up to one side of the penalty area and the coach stands on the other. The first player dribbles with the ball and then plays a firm pass to the coach who returns the ball into the penalty area. The player should then sprint to the ball, set himself and shoot at goal. Ensure the players put maximum effort into the sprint, as they will get plenty of recovery before the next effort. Each player should repeat the exercise six to seven times.

Speed and agility

Players start in groups either side of a small goal or cones set up to replicate a small goal. A cone is placed 20m away in line with the middle of the goal. When the coach calls 'go', the front two players sprint around the cone and back to the ball. The first one there shoots to score. Each player repeats the drill approximately six to seven times.

Small-sided game

82. Small-sided fitness games – 4 v 4 or 5 v 5 (20–25 mins)
Set-up
Set up as a small-sided game. The drill involves working with three teams – two play and one does fitness conditioning as set by the coach.

Drill flow
Teams play for 4–5 minutes. Teams who are playing must play at a high tempo. The team not playing sprints or jogs the short sides of the area and then recovers on the long lengths or vice versa. After 4–5 minutes' play the losing team go outside to run.

Key factors
■ Ensure that games are at as high a tempo as possible.
■ Introduce conditions to the game, i.e. passes below head height, two touch, one touch etc.
■ Ensure the two teams in the middle are playing at a high tempo. If one team or a player does not, swap them to the outside. This should motivate the two playing teams to keep the tempo up, working them harder than the running players.
■ The players running around the outside should sprint either one long or short length (this choice is the coach's). They then use the other length to recover with either a slow jog or walk. Ensure the sprints are at maximum output.

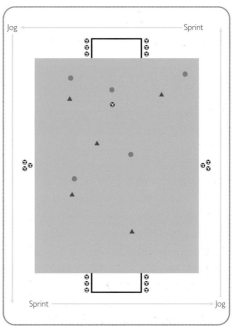

Small-sided game

83. Small-sided fitness games – 7 v 7 or 8 v 8 (20–25 mins)

Set-up

Set up as a small-sided game. The drill involves working with two or three teams (if there are three, two should play while one rests).

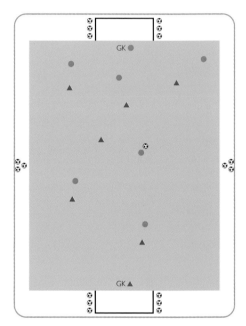

Drill flow

Teams play for 4–5 minutes. Those playing must play at a high tempo. Conditions are set to overload the teams. Set penalties for the losing teams.

Key factors

- Introduce conditions to the game, i.e. passes below head height, two touch, one touch, a minimum amount of passes before the team can score etc.
- Introduce conditions such as, if a team scores, the whole team must sprint around the goal they scored in and then get back on to the field of play, while at the same time allowing the third team (if you have three teams) to get on to the pitch. Maybe if a player loses the ball he has to sprint around a goal before he can re-enter the game, or if a ball goes off, the player who caused it to go off must get the ball back (have enough balls so that the opposition team can get another and begin play to create an overload).
- Keep the conditions such that you keep trying to overload one team or the other to make the overloaded team work harder.
- Have a penalty at the end of the games for the team that finishes last (give three points for a win and one for a draw). Ensure that no team wants to lose (otherwise they get two laps around the pitch followed by press-ups, sit-ups etc).

fitness testing

Technical practice

84. Fitness testing session (time varies depending on age/ability)

Performance in any sporting event is the result of a number of different factors, which can include the amount of training performed, the motivation levels of the player and weather conditions to name just a few. By carrying out coordinated fitness testing, levels of fitness can be measured and hence improved upon.

The ultimate test of a player's fitness capability is game performance – this is the best indication of training success. It is important to determine the players' starting levels and monitor their improvements so that you can see the areas of development and can modify training programmes if necessary. Carrying out an initial test or series of tests will give you an idea of where players' fitness levels are at the start of a programme and subsequent testing will give a good idea of the effectiveness of the training programme. The time frame between tests will depend on the availability of time or the phase of training the players occupy. This may range from between two weeks and six months, however, bear in mind that a minimum of two to six weeks may be required to see a demonstrable change in any aspect of their fitness.

Bleep test (time varies depending on age/ability)

The bleep test, or multi-stage fitness test, is employed by many international sporting teams as an accurate test of cardiovascular fitness, one of the most important components of fitness. It involves running continuously between two points 20m apart. These runs are synchronised with a pre-recorded series of beeps, which play at set intervals. As the test proceeds, the interval between each successive beep reduces, forcing the athlete to increase velocity over the course of the test, until it is impossible to keep in sync with the recording.

Fig. 06:04 Bleep test

The recording is typically structured into 23 levels, each of which lasts around 63 seconds (the shortest is level 1, lasting 59.29 seconds, the longest is level 8, lasting 66 seconds). Usually, the interval of beeps requires a speed at the start of 8.5 km/h, increasing by 0.5 km/h with each level. Players must reach the end of the 20m course before the next beep and are normally allowed three failures to do this before they are scored for the test.

The progression from one level to the next is signalled by three rapid beeps. The highest level attained by the player before they fail for the third time is recorded as the score for that test.

The audio for a bleep test can be found and purchased from a number of different sites on the web in CD, DVD or downloadable formats.

Cooper test (time varies depending on age/ability)

The Cooper test is another cardiovascular fitness test and is carried out around the perimeter of a football pitch. Before conducting the test, you need to mark out the pitch so that the distance covered can be recorded. This may be done at set distances of, say, 50m, or you may use the marking of the pitch along with middle marker cones along the width of the pitch. Players then run/walk for 12 minutes and at the end the distance covered is measured and recorded.

Fig. 06:05 The Cooper test: indicative measurements of performance

Age	Excellent	Above average	Average	Below average	Poor
Males 13–14	>2700m	2400–2700m	2200–2399m	2100–2199m	<2100m
Females 13–14	>2000m	1900–2000m	1600–1899m	1500–1599m	<1500m
Males 15–16	>2800m	2500–2800m	2300–2499m	2200–2299m	<2200m
Females 15–16	>2100m	2000–2100m	1700–1999m	1600–1699m	<1600m
Males 17–19	>3000m	2700–3000m	2500–2699m	2300–2499m	<2300m
Females 17–19	>2300m	2100–2300m	1800–2099m	1700–1799m	<1700m

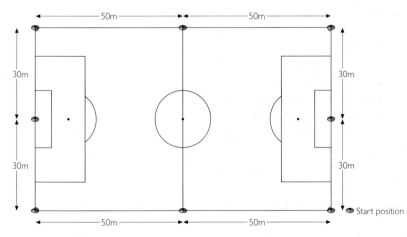

Sprint test

A sprint test assesses maximum running speed and is measured over a 40m distance. Use marker cones, a stopwatch, recording media and, ideally, an assistant to record the results. Each player has three runs – record their fastest time.

Fig. 06:06 Sprint test

part three
protecting your best assets

07
Child protection and safety

It is a sad fact that many children are abused sexually, emotionally or physically. As a soccer coach you are in a unique position to spot any signs of abuse among your players and it is vital, therefore, that you are able to recognise the signs of abuse and know what to do if you suspect anything untoward is occurring. Everyone who has a role in working with children has a moral and legal responsibility to safeguard and promote a child's welfare, particularly when it comes to protecting children from abuse. Therefore, as a coach you need to ensure that the players are not subjected to bullying or criticism in front of their peers. You must also make sure that you do not expose your players to extremes of weather, leave them unsupervised, make or force them to play when they have been injured or train them in an over-intense way or in a way that is inappropriate to their age. Remember that the safety and welfare of children should always be of paramount importance, whatever the circumstances.

Ideally, if you are coaching at a club or organisation it should have a Child Protection Policy that ensures that the welfare and safety of children in the care or custody of that club or organisation is always the primary consideration. It should also have a Child Protection Coordinator who can advise on current policy and procedures in relation to child protection and should be the first point of contact for all coaches, parents, guardians or others regarding concerns for the welfare of any child or young player. In the UK, where the individual FAs have worked hard in this area, it is now required that every youth club has a person in charge of child welfare, called a Child Welfare Officer (CWO).

If no such policy exists or if you want to provide such a policy, below is an example for our sample club City Rovers.

City Rovers Child Protection Policy

City Rovers have committed to providing an environment where children can learn about, participate in and enjoy soccer free from harassment or abuse.

The club policy states that it will strive to develop a positive and proactive position in order to best protect all children and young people who play soccer, enabling them to participate in an enjoyable and safe environment. The club will also deliver quality assured child protection and provide a strong tutor network within the club in conjunction with its local Football Association and Council and ensure that all coaching staff attend a national Child Protection and Working With Children course to make sure they are all conversant with the latest child protection policies and methodology.

The child's welfare is, and must always be, the paramount consideration. All children and young people have a right to be protected from abuse regardless of their age, gender, disability, culture, racial origin, religious beliefs or sexual identity. All allegations and suspicions of abuse will be taken seriously and responded to swiftly and appropriately.

The club has applied and issued procedures for protecting children to all managers and coaches and has the following guidelines on how to deal with disclosures to them:

- Do not promise confidentiality.
- Explain who you will tell and why.
- Listen to what is being said, without displaying shock or disbelief.
- Accept what is being said.
- Allow the child to talk freely and limit any questions to a minimum. Seek only to clarify and strictly avoid leading the child or adult who has made the approach by making suggestions or introducing their own ideas into what may have happened.
- Never ask questions such as 'did X do Y to you?' Instead use a minimum of prompts of the 'tell me what happened' type.
- If it is an adult making the approach and it becomes obvious that they are making a significant allegation concerning either abuse or neglect, the club's Club Welfare Officer (CWO) should be contacted to avoid repetition of details.
- Be especially careful to distinguish between fact and opinion. Note also any non-verbal behaviour.
- Reassure the child, but do not make promises you cannot keep. Reassure the child that what has happened to them is not their fault.
- Stress that the child has done the right thing in telling you.
- Do not agree with the child by condemning or criticising the perpetrator.

Make a factual record of the events that includes the following and pass to the club CWO, local or national child protection service or their local or national Football Association:

- ▸ The child's name, address and date of birth.
- ▸ The nature of the allegation, who was involved and what happened.
- ▸ A description of any visible bruising and injuries.
- ▸ The child's or young person's account (in their words) of what happened.
- ▸ Any observations they have made, or have been made to them.

- ▸ Any times, places, dates or other relevant information.
- ▸ A clear distinction of what is fact, opinion and hearsay.
- ▸ Your knowledge of and relationship to the child or young person.

If any member of the coaching staff at any stage has concerns for their own safety, especially owing to them having made a referral, they should immediately contact the CWO who will promptly involve the appropriate bodies.

By following the above procedure, the coach is protecting themselves and the club/organisation.

Promoting good practice

Child abuse, particularly sexual abuse, can arouse strong emotions in those facing such a situation. It is important to understand these feelings and not allow them to interfere with your judgement about the appropriate action to take.

Abuse can occur within many situations including the home, school and the sporting environment. Some individuals will actively seek employment or voluntary work with young people in order to harm them. A coach, instructor, teacher, official or volunteer will have regular contact with young people and be an important link in identifying cases where they need protection.

When a child enters a soccer club or organisation having been subjected to child abuse outside the sporting environment, sport can play a crucial role in improving the child's self-esteem. In such instances the club must work with the appropriate agencies to ensure the child receives the required support.

Good practice guidelines

All personnel should be encouraged to demonstrate exemplary behaviour in order to protect themselves from false allegations. The following are common sense examples of how to create a positive culture and climate.

Good practice means:

- Always working in an open environment avoiding private or unobserved situations and encouraging open communication.
- Treating all young people with respect and dignity.
- Always putting the welfare of each young person first.
- Maintaining a safe and appropriate distance with players (e.g. it is not appropriate for staff or volunteers to have an intimate relationship with a child or to share a room with them).
- Building balanced relationships based on mutual trust and empowering children to share in decision-making.

- Making sport fun, enjoyable and promoting fair play.
- Keeping up to date with technical skills, qualifications and insurance.
- Involving parents/carers wherever possible. For example, encouraging them to take responsibility for their children in the changing rooms. If groups have to be supervised in the changing rooms, always ensure parents, teachers, coaches or officials work in pairs.
- Ensuring that if mixed teams are taken away for the day or night a male and female member of staff always accompanies them. However, remember that same gender abuse can also occur.
- Ensuring that at tournaments or residential events adults should not enter children's rooms or invite children into their rooms.
- Being an excellent role model – this includes not smoking or drinking alcohol in the company of young people.
- Giving enthusiastic and constructive feedback rather than negative criticism.
- Recognising the developmental needs and capacity of young people – avoiding excessive training or competition and not pushing them against their will.
- Securing parental consent in writing to act in loco parentis, if the need arises to administer emergency first aid and/or other medical treatment.
- Keeping a written record of any injury that occurs, along with the details of any treatment given.
- Requesting written parental consent if club officials are required to transport young people in their cars.

Practices to be avoided

The following should be avoided, except in emergencies. If a case arises where these situations are unavoidable (e.g. the child sustains an injury and needs to go to hospital, or a parent fails to arrive to pick a child up at the end of a session), it should be with the full knowledge and consent of someone in charge in the club/organisation or the child's parents.

- Spending excessive amounts of time alone with children away from others.
- Taking or dropping off a child to an event.

Practices never to be sanctioned

The following should never be sanctioned. You should never:

- Engage in rough physical or sexually provocative games, including horseplay.
- Share a room with a child.
- Allow or engage in any form of inappropriate touching.
- Allow children to use inappropriate language unchallenged.

- Make sexually suggestive comments to a child, even in fun.
- Reduce a child to tears as a form of control.
- Allow allegations made by a child to go unchallenged, unrecorded or not acted upon.
- Do things of a personal nature for children that they can do for themselves.
- Invite or allow children to stay with you at your home unsupervised.

Sometimes it may be necessary for you as a coach to do things of a personal nature for children, particularly if they are young or are disabled. These tasks should only be carried out with the full understanding and consent of parents and the players involved. There is a need to be responsive to a person's reactions. If a person is fully dependent on you, talk with them about what you are doing and give choices where possible. This is particularly so if you are involved in any dressing or undressing of outer clothing, or where there is physical contact, lifting or assisting a child to carry out particular activities. Avoid taking on the responsibility for tasks for which you are not appropriately trained.

Reporting incidents or accidents
If any of the following occur you should report this immediately to another colleague and record the incident. You should also ensure the parents of the child are informed:

- If you accidentally hurt a player.
- If he/she seems distressed in any manner.
- If a player appears to be sexually aroused by your actions.
- If a player misunderstands or misinterprets something you have done.

Use of photographic equipment at sporting events
There is evidence that some people have used sporting events as an opportunity to take inappropriate photographs or film footage of young and disabled sportspeople in vulnerable positions. All clubs/organisations should be vigilant and any concerns should to be reported to the club and, if they have one, to their CWO. If playing against another team, approval should always be asked for, and granted from, the opposition team before any images are taken. If this approval is denied, NO photographic equipment should be used.

Bullying
A lot of young people have a good idea of what bullying is because they see it every day. Bullying happens when someone hurts or scares another person on purpose, and the person being bullied has a hard time defending themselves. Usually, bullying

is not confined to a one-off event, but happens over and over again. Bullying can take the form of, but is not exclusively limited to:

- Punching, shoving and other acts that hurt people physically.
- Spreading bad rumours about people.
- Keeping certain people out of a 'group'.
- Teasing people in a mean way.
- Getting certain people to 'gang up' on others.

In today's technical age, bullying also can happen online or electronically. Cyber bullying is becoming more and more common and happens when children or teens bully each other using the Internet, mobile phones or other technology. Again this can take the form of, but is not exclusively limited to:

- Sending offensive texts, e-mails or instant messages.
- Posting offensive pictures or messages about others in blogs or on websites.
- Using someone else's user name to spread rumours or lies about someone.

Unfortunately, not everyone takes bullying seriously, including adults, however as a coach, you should:

- Take all signs of bullying very seriously.
- Encourage all children to speak and share their concerns. Help the victim to speak out and tell the person in charge or someone in authority.
- Investigate all allegations and take action to ensure the victim is safe.
- Speak with the victim and the person or people who are carrying out the bullying separately.
- Reassure the victim that you can be trusted and will help them, although you cannot promise to tell no one else.
- Keep records of what is said (what happened, by whom, when).
- Where possible, report any concerns to the CPO/CWO or your club/ organisation.

With regards to the person or persons carrying out the bullying, as a coach you should:

- Talk with the bully or bullies, explain the situation, and try to get them to understand the consequences of their behaviour. Seek an apology to the victim(s).
- Inform the bully's parents.

- Insist on the return of 'borrowed' items and that the bullies compensate the victim.
- Impose sanctions as necessary.
- Encourage and support the bullies to change behaviour.
- Hold meetings with the families to report on progress.
- Keep a written record of action taken.
- Where possible, inform the CPO/CWO of all action taken.

08
Mental and physiological development

The importance of sport psychology in football is becoming increasingly well recognised with many professional clubs now employing a sports psychologist. In years gone by, sport psychology could well have been referred to as mental preparation, mind games, or mind over matter. All have the same meaning and aims, which is for the team to achieve a peak performance in every match.

Sport psychology or mental preparation is another tool for a coach to use to prepare players for a game, however, they should realise that it is no substitute for skills. The main aim of psychological preparation is to attain peak performance, so it will not help much if the team's performance is poor; it is vital to emphasise that this is an additional tool and is no substitute for skill.

To emphasise the benefits of sports psychology, as a coach, have you ever heard comments about a player who should have played at a higher level but 'didn't have the bottle' or 'choked in the big games', or have you heard the phrases 'makes use of his limited talent', 'has a great work ethic' or 'never gives up'? These comments are simply statements about a player's mental qualities.

Think about professional players or even teams. Until winning the Euro Championships in 2008, the Spanish team was always seen as full of potential but always underachieved or 'choked' on the big occasion. Look at players in high pressure situations such as penalty shoot outs who have stepped up to take their kick and looked so nervous that it seemed obvious they would miss. All of this can be down to stress, anxiety or fear of failure.

As a coach, being able to identify the different mental qualities of all of your players will allow you to understand what motivates each player or causes them to get anxious. You can set strategies for both training sessions and games to allow each player and the team to achieve maximum levels of performance. The effective coach will understand the four key mental qualities and work out strategies for dealing with them.

Table 08.01 Four key mental qualities		
Mental quality	Positive examples	Negative examples
1. Confidence	• Wants to be on the ball • Is willing to take on opponents in 1 v 1 situations both defensively and offensively • Strong communicator with positive calls and use of encouragement	• Does not get involved or goes missing • Avoids contact or tackles • Hesitates on shooting chances, or avoids them • Plays with their head down and passes poorly
2. Commitment	• Has a great work ethic and plays with maximum effort • Looks to win the ball in contact situations and has the belief they always will • Does not complain at being asked to play in a new position, or works hard on mastering new techniques	• Is late for training or does not turn up at all • When at training or matches does not give 100 per cent effort • Is not concerned with personal or team performance and shows lack of interest
3. Concentration	• Does not get distracted by parents, spectators or opposition players • Does not get distracted by own mistakes or poor efforts and remains focused • Does not get distracted by stoppages in play	• Worries about pitch conditions, weather conditions or amount of spectators • Is easily wound up by opposition or comments from spectators • Lacks focus after a poor pass or technical mistake
4. Composure	• Does not retaliate to fouls or abuse, but remains calm • Remains calm when shooting or having an effort on goal • Remains calm when defending a set piece	• Shows outbursts of emotion after making a mistake • Argues or abuses teammates, referees, coaching staff or spectators • Is irritable, moody or argumentative

These key mental qualities can often be interlinked, for instance a player who is low in confidence may well lack composure and lose concentration. They may also suffer from other psychological symptoms such as anxiety or arousal.

Anxiety and arousal

Anxiety and arousal can often be confused as meaning the same thing, such as the heightened feelings of physical and mental nervousness experienced when a player's stress levels increase prior to an important game.

Arousal, however, is the physical response to increased stress or pressure and will often result in sweaty palms, dry mouths, increased heart rate and butterflies in the stomach. These are normal responses to heightened pressure and often a player will seek to increase their own levels of arousal to get them ready or tuned in for the game. As a coach, you should look to use the warm-up to promote an increased level of mental arousal and physical readiness.

Anxiety also leads to a heightened level of mental and physical responses. When the level of pressure is increased, however, it will often have a negative impact on performance. While pressure can focus the mind of players and prepare them for a game, if the pressure becomes too much, the player could become physically and emotionally anxious. This anxiousness can lead to self-doubt, tension, worry or fear. When any or all of these physical or emotional issues arise, the chances are performance will be negatively affected. Players, who are anxious while playing in games, may well lose focus, concentrate too much on their own performance and not see the runs or hear the calls from their teammates, their decision-making may well be impaired and they could play with a lack of vision, or end up ball-watching.

As a coach, it is important that you are able to detect those players who get anxious before a game and those players who need to be psyched up before a game. The anxious players will need to be reassured and calmed down, focused on their own strengths and understanding their own weaknesses and dealing with them, probably on a one to one basis. Rather than psyching up the whole team, which may generate unwanted anxiety in some players, take aside those players that need psyching up and deal with them as a separate group.

Table 08:02 Examples of physical and emotional anxiety	
Physical signs of anxiety	Emotional signs of anxiety
Sickness (feeling sick or actually being sick)	Worry or fear at losing the game or their place in the team
Headaches and/or muscle tension	Negative thoughts such as 'I never play well against these . . .' or 'I'll never be able to cope with that player'
Increased sweating and heart rate	Self-criticism such as 'I'm no good at . . .'
Shaking or trembling	Short attention span, lack of attention, lack of focus

Self-esteem

It is important to realise that in youth players often their own sense of value, worth and social standing with their peers is very important to them. Football can often be a valuable source of self-esteem for an adolescent teenager and it is vital as a coach that you recognise this and be mindful of the fragile emotional development that a youth player undergoes during this time. All players are people and they need to be encouraged to turn into better football players, and confident and responsible young adults. Remember to make them feel valued and part of the team, liked and with a sense of worth, regardless of their playing ability, and to feel confident and competent in their efforts.

Confidence

Confidence is one of the key mental qualities that a coach should work on. If players are confident in their own abilities, they will be motivated, assured, composed and focused on their roles and responsibilities within the team. They should avoid the negative effects of anxiety and, in general, play to their highest ability in training and games. The confident player will not let poor performance affect them and will persevere in their endeavours. They will attempt to do things to improve themselves and accept challenges outside their own personal comfort zone. They will be positive and encourage others within the team and stand up and be counted for their own personal and team performances.

Players who lack confidence will also more than likely have low self-esteem. They will overreact to the amount of blame they put on themselves, or refuse to accept any form of blame and instead blame others. They will lack enthusiasm and have negative comments on their own and the team's performance. They may remove themselves from games, due to perceived injuries or tiredness, and will not push themselves in training or games. As important as it is to spot anxiousness in players, it is also important to spot a lack of confidence and work with players to improve this. How do we deal with all of these issues?

Communication is the best way to improve and maintain a player's confidence, self-esteem and self-worth. Can you work together with the player and their parents or guardians to improve this confidence? How often have you seen over zealous parents dampen a player's confidence or self-esteem with their overcritical

Table 08:03 Improving confidence in football situations – coach and player		
Football scenario	Player's actions	Coach's actions
Feeling low in confidence due to poor performances	• Set themselves realistic goals to achieve • Focus on technical goals rather than performance goals (e.g. improve runs on and off the ball as opposed to score two goals)	• Re-set the player's goals to allow for a gradual improvement towards these targets and share with the player and their parents • Ensure the player can see this improvement in the practices, but also make sure once they understand, you push them on to challenge them
Playing against bigger or stronger opponents	• Replaying in their own minds, examples of when they achieved success in such situations before	• Reinforcing the player's strengths and skills through practice and communication • Working on a strategy to meet the challenge (pass and move to avoid contact)
Trying to develop a new technique or skill	• Being positive in their belief that they can master this skill • Watch another player of similar ability perform the technique	• Reinforce this positive belief by providing positive feedback • Work players of similar ability together with one showing the other how it is done

comments or advice? Can you set players' targets and then work with the parents or guardians to communicate how they are doing against these targets, and the progress they are making along with their strengths?

By doing this, you are keeping all parties informed and this should reduce tensions and ease any frictions. By setting realistic targets, you are not only setting out what is required of the player, but you are also keeping the parents' or guardians' perceptions and expectations on the correct level, and they are not aspiring to a level of performance that their child cannot deliver. If an issue does arise where conflict is possible with parents, avoid carrying this out in front of the player. Talk to them directly rather than through the player or write or e-mail them to explain your actions, decisions or thoughts. Always be as truthful and frank as possible; if bad news needs delivering, do it sensitively, avoid negative or harsh comments and always try and offer a plan on how the player can continue to develop. Finally, remember you can never please everyone and in trying to do so, you may eventually upset all.

Develop a player profile

To allow you to continually monitor your player's mental characteristics, develop a player profile for each player. By defining these mental characteristics, you can then prepare a development plan for improving your squad's mental skills and qualities. Once completed, share the profile with each of the players, agree on the assessment or amend it where necessary, and then work on improving it with the player.

See opposite for an example of such a player profile and a template for your own use.

Fig. 08:04 Player profile sample

Player name: Jamie Fisher
Position: Midfield
Date: 12th September

Quality	Ideal player (IP)	Coach's assessment of actual player (CA)	Area for development (AD) (AD=IP-CA)
Confidence	10	7	3
Motivation	10	7	3
Commitment	10	10	0
Concentration	10	8	2
Awareness/vision	10	8	2
Arousal	10	6	4
Anxiety	10	4	6

Player profile template

Player name:
Position:
Date:

Quality	Ideal player (IP)	Coach's assessment of actual player (CA)	Area for development (AD) (AD=IP-CA)
Confidence			
Motivation			
Commitment			
Concentration			
Awareness/vision			
Arousal			
Anxiety			

Coach's mental qualities

The mental qualities that a player has will determine how they react and perform in a game and will be the difference between success and failure but, as a coach, we also need to be mindful of our own mental qualities and how these will rub off on the players and affect their performance.

Below is a guide to the mental qualities a coach should exhibit and the actions that spring from them:

Table 08:04 Coach's mental qualities		
Period	Mental quality	Actions required
On the way to the game	Confidence	Use positive statements to reinforce and restate the goals and targets for the game, outwardly show a state of quiet confidence in the team's capabilities
Arrival at the game	Composure (emotional control)	Use positive statements as above, take care of pre-game needs, e.g. kit etc, reassure anxious players
During the warm-up	Concentration	Avoid irrelevant information or giving too much information. Keep comments simple and focused on the tasks and goals
At half-time	Confidence and composure	Use encouraging and constructive statements, avoid distractions and focus on the key goals for the next period of play
During the game	Confidence and concentration	Keep instructions brief and focused, don't overload the players with information, use trigger words to focus attention

09

Coach, player and parental codes of conduct

Often a coach's personal beliefs will be placed under pressure by other coaches, players, officials and spectators due to these people's interpretations of the laws of the game and their own views on acceptable levels of behaviour. This becomes even more relevant when a match is of a high level of importance and others may believe that, due to the rewards on offer, the stretching of the laws is more acceptable.

As a coach it is our job to reinforce the importance of the laws of the game, as they have been developed, to ensure fairness and equality. These laws enable the game to be played and any player who deliberately flouts these laws destroys the whole essence of the game.

If you think back to the worst games you have experienced, these were probably the games where the laws were infringed the most and the behaviour of certain groups of people were the most unacceptable, be it the players, officials or parents/spectators.

While it is very difficult to control the actions and behaviour of opposition players, officials and spectators, by imposing codes of conduct for your own players, parents and club officials, you can ensure that your team's behaviour is to a high standard and one which hopefully will show other teams how they 'could' be.

By promoting fair play, high standards of behaviour and the highest level of coaching conduct possible, you will not only set yourselves out as role models for other teams, you will show prospective players and parents the standards your team adopts and what they could expect if they brought their children to your team.

Coach's code of conduct

Every player within your team can expect you, as their coach, to adhere to a coaching code of conduct. If your club does not have such a code of conduct, below is an example for our sample club City Rovers.

City Rovers Coach's Code of Conduct

City Rovers coaches are required to abide by the code of conduct set out below:

- Coaches must respect the rights, dignity and worth of each and every person and treat each equally within the context of the sport.

- Coaches must place the well-being and safety of each player above all other considerations, including the development of performance.
- Coaches must adhere to all guidelines laid down by the FA and the Rules of the Football Association.
- Coaches must develop an appropriate working relationship with each player based on mutual trust and respect.
- Coaches must not exert undue influence to obtain personal benefit or reward.
- Coaches must encourage and guide players to accept responsibility for their own behaviour and performance.
- Coaches must ensure that the activities they direct or advocate are appropriate for the age, maturity, experience and ability of players.
- Coaches should, at the outset, clarify with the player (and, where appropriate, their parents) exactly what is expected of them and also what they are entitled to expect from their coach.
- Coaches must cooperate fully with other specialists (e.g. other coaches, officials, sports scientists, doctors, physiotherapists) in the best interests of the player.
- Coaches must always promote the positive aspects of the sport (e.g. fair play) and never condone violations of the laws of the game, behaviour contrary to the spirit of the laws of the game or relevant rules and regulations, or the use of prohibited substances or techniques.
- Coaches must consistently display high standards of behaviour and appearance.

Next you should ensure that a players and parental code of conduct is in place. Again, if your club does not have such a code of conduct, below is an example for our sample club City Rovers.

Players and Parental Code of Conduct
City Rovers have the following code of conduct for their parents and players, to which they are expected to adhere:
    'Wear The Shirt With Pride'

- Players should to be on their best behaviour at all times when representing the club. This includes training sessions and travelling to and from games as well as at matches themselves.
- Players will always promote goodwill by acting in a sportsmanlike way and shaking hands with the opposition and referee after every game; regardless of the result.
- Players are expected to give of their best at all times and to support their manager/coach and teammates at all times.
- Always listen quietly and attentively to what your manager/coach tells you.

- Comments to others should always be constructive and positive and must never be personal.
- Parents should leave the coaching of the team and the tactics to the manager/coach. Too many contradictory instructions can simply confuse players.
- The referee's decision is always final and should never be argued with.
- Foul or abusive language will not be tolerated under any circumstances.
- The club kit and equipment should always be treated with respect. Kit should always be washed/cleaned after each match and remains the property of the club. It must not be used for any other activities.
- Winning is not everything! Accept victory humbly and defeat graciously.
- Players and club officials should always respect the referee and officials.

Over and above this player/parental code of conduct, you may wish to ask your players to adhere to a team code of conduct for both training and matches. The following is an example:

Player Code of Conduct

Training

1 I will arrive promptly at training sessions and be ready to train for the start of the session.
2 I will not bring people or items to training that will distract me from training.
3 Training is designed to allow me to develop my ability in terms of skill, technique, tactics and stamina. I will therefore be attentive during training and, to the best of my ability, help other players to develop.
4 I will give my maximum effort during training and strive to produce the best possible performance I can to help improve my own standards and that of my teammates.
5 I will set a positive example for others within my team and outside of my team.
6 I will avoid all forms of gamesmanship and time wasting.
7 I will not use inappropriate language and accept that foul or abusive language will not be tolerated under any circumstances.
8 I will encourage other players within the team and will not make fun or otherwise upset them.
9 If I am not in a position to do the above, I will not attend training and accept that potentially I will not be selected for the next game.

Matches

1 I will arrive promptly for matches and be ready to play. Where I need to get ready for a game, I will do so in a prompt manner allowing me to warm up properly prior to the game.

2 I will not bring people or items to matches that will distract me from playing.

3 I will give my maximum effort and strive to give the best possible performance during a game, even if our team is in a position where the desired result has already been achieved or where the game is effectively beyond winning.

4 I will set a positive example for others within my team and outside of my team.

5 I will avoid all forms of gamesmanship and time wasting.

6 I will not use inappropriate language and accept that foul or abusive language will not be tolerated under any circumstances.

7 I will encourage other players within the team and will not make fun or otherwise upset them.

8 I will always have regard for the best interests of the game, including where publicly expressing an opinion on the game or any particular aspect of it, including others within the game.

9 I will abide by the laws, rules and spirit of the game and make every effort to play in a spirit of fair play.

10 I will accept the decisions of match officials without protest and will treat them in a respectful manner, whether I agree with their decisions or not.

11 I will treat opponents with due respect at all times, irrespective of the result of the game.

12 While winning is important, I will accept victory humbly and defeat graciously.

Soccer Parent

Soccer Parent is an initiative designed by the English FA. With coaches and parents in mind, it aims to provide guidance on specific areas, focusing on the key issues involved when a child joins a football team.

As well as being designed to be informative, fun and engaging, one of the key aspects of the course is that coaches are given advice to assist in gaining positive contributions from parents, as well as understanding issues on specific areas such as child welfare and attitudes.

Soccer Parent is a completely free online course that is available to anybody that registers with the English FA Learning – The English FA's Educational Provider. Everyone that completes the course and achieves the pass mark can immediately print off an accredited certificate directly from the website.

Simply go to www.thefa.com and click on the 'grassroots' tab at the top of the site and then on the link to 'parents'.

Appendix

The coach's future development and learning

One of the underpinning values of a good coach is their desire to continually improve themselves, to be open to innovative and new ideas and to look for outside support to help them to develop their players.

Below is a summary of the different courses that you as a coach can look to take to develop your own personal skills:

European coaches courses

UEFA C Licence Equivalent to the English FA's Level 2 qualification. Suitable for coaches looking to coach players up to the age of 12–14

UEFA B Licence Equivalent to the English FA's Level 3 qualification. Suitable for coaches looking to coach players up to the age of 16–18

UEFA A Licence Suitable for coaches looking to coach players above the age of 18

North American coaches courses

National C Licence Suitable for coaches looking to coach players from the age of 11–14

National B Licence Suitable for coaches looking to coach players from the age of 16 to college level

National A Licence Suitable for coaches looking to coach players from post-college to adult levels

Online coaching resources

English FA's website
www.thefa.com

European Football Association
www.uefa.com

Football Federation International Governing Body
www.fifa.com

USA Soccer Federation
www.ussoccer.com

Index